Public Sector Economics

Public Sector Economics

Papers presented at the 1967 Section F
meeting of the British Association for the
Advancement of Science

Edited by A R Prest

Manchester University Press

Published by
Manchester University Press
316–324 Oxford Road
Manchester 13

GB SBN 7190 0330 X

Printed by Butler & Tanner Ltd
Frome and London

Contents

Contents

Introductory note

It was decided to organize the papers presented at the 1967 Section F meeting of the British Association for the Advancement of Science in Leeds around the general area of Public Sector Economics. This volume brings together the papers, more or less as presented, in the hope that they may be of interest to a wider audience. They are reproduced in the order in which they were given at the meeting.

I am grateful to the editors of the *Economics Journal* for permission to reproduce the first paper.

A R Prest

Manchester
November 1967

1

A R Prest

Sense and nonsense in budgetary policy

When I think of the long line of eminent men who have
delivered a presidential address to Section F—I observe that,
for instance, Alfred Marshall spoke at the Leeds meeting in
1890 on 'Some aspects of competition' and D. H. Macgregor at
the 1927 meeting in Leeds on 'Rationalization in industry'—I
can only reflect with sadness on the decline in standards
evidenced by my filling this position. The contrast is further
heightened by the increase in the prestige of the social sciences
generally, and that of economics in particular, over the years.
To illustrate this, there is the delightful story about the 1870s
in Lady Longford's biography of Queen Victoria.[1] A party of
social scientists asked to be allowed to visit Balmoral in 1877.
The Queen gave instructions that they could be allowed in the
grounds but not on any account in the house itself. She sub-
sequently asked Sir Henry Ponsonby what they were like and
had the reply that he had seldom seen a slummier lot. One
likes to think that the standing of social scientists, deservedly
or undeservedly, is a little higher today.

My concern is to look at some of the major themes of
budgetary policy in this country over the last twenty years or
so and try to highlight lessons which should have been learned
from these experiences. I should like to amplify this statement
in several ways. Firstly, I am using the word 'budgetary' as a
short-hand for 'revenue and expenditure'. My coverage will
therefore be wider than what is often implied by the term
'fiscal' policy: on the other hand, I shall not trench on the many

[1] Elizabeth Longford, *Victoria R.I.* (Weidenfeld & Nicolson, London,
1964), p. 420.

1

other issues, e.g. monetary policy, controls on overseas capital movements and so on, which Chancellors of the Exchequer frequently discuss in their budget speeches. Secondly, I am taking a highly subjective view: I am not bold enough to say what lessons have been learned but am only putting forward my view, with which many may disagree, about what ought to have been learned. Thirdly, with a subject as vast as this, I must be highly selective if I am to satisfy the time constraint. I shall in fact concentrate on the following three themes: the adjustment of aggregate demand and supply; investment stimuli; and particular tax concessions and subsidies.

It will at once be obvious that there are many important topics (e.g. social security) which I shall not cover at all and that, even so, some of my remarks will perforce be of a very general, not to say superficial, character.

I

If one had to select a single point of time from which it could be said that henceforth a guiding principle of budgetary policy in this country should be the adjustment of aggregate demand to aggregate supply, the choice would almost certainly be Sir Kingsley Wood's Budget of 1941, with its explicit references to the need to judge proposals for tax increases in the light of the prospective inflationary gap.[1] It is no secret that Keynes played a major part in formulating these ideas; and it is also no secret that the ideas were somewhat beyond the Chancellor.[2] However, by the end of the war the general principles were widely accepted and already enshrined in such classic documents as Beveridge's *Full Employment in a Free Society*[3] and the 1944 White Paper.[4] Indeed, at that time it was sometimes asserted

[1] Hansard (Commons) 1940-1, vol. 370, cols. 1297-1335.

[2] One hard-bitten parliamentary observer of the time is alleged to have said that he had on many occasions listened to speeches by ministers which they had not written; but this was the first time he had heard a speech which the minister had neither written nor understood.

[3] Beveridge, *Full Employment in a Free Society* (Allen & Unwin, London, 1944). [4] *Employment Policy*, Cmd. 6527, HMSO, London, 1944.

that the regulation of overall demand relative to supply was the only budget principle that really mattered and that, furthermore, it was a comparatively easy principle to put into effect. In re-reading some of the early post-war economic surveys and budget speeches, one is struck by the confidence of the authors that they could estimate prospective demand in the year ahead, the likely supply potential and the likely inflationary gap—at a time when national accounts were far less detailed than they are today, when there was no adequate official index of industrial production, no up-to-date census of production, no surveys of intended private capital expenditure and so on.[1] It was in reality a classic case of the belief that faith could move mountains. Some sceptics raised their voices in disbelief at the more extravagant claims[2] but, by and large, it seems fair to characterize the predominant view of the time as roughly 101% certain of the rightness of the principles of Keynesian fiscal policy and 99% certain of their practicality.

What in reality has been our experience in this country? Clearly one cannot summarize in a few words the economic history of a major country over a twenty-year period and so the following remarks do no more than touch the top of a very large iceberg. The first observation is surely that we have been extraordinarily successful in maintaining full employment, whether judged by the standards of the past or by those of other countries. To keep at least 97% (and sometimes as much as 99%) of the working population in employment over a twenty-year period is an achievement in which we really can take pride. Unfortunately the employment percentage is not the only test of policy success. As Sir Roy Harrod has recently pointed out, the relatively stable percentage employment figures conceal much larger fluctuations in industrial production.[3] The balance of payments crises and the gyrations

[1] In fairness, one should add that some private activities were very much dependent on public controls and so forecasts could be made on that basis.

[2] See, for instance, Sir Hubert Henderson, *The Uses and Abuses of Economic Planning* (Cambridge University Press, 1947).

[3] E.g. whereas from 1955 last quarter to 1958 last quarter industrial

of the economy in the successive phases of 'stop' and 'go', the low growth rate of output and the high growth rate of prices are too well known to require documentation in detail. Nor is there any convincing evidence that forecasting of prospective crises—or at any rate appropriate action emanating from accurate forecasts—has improved over the period. At the beginning of the period, we had the severe crisis of summer 1947 followed by the devaluation of September 1949; and at the end we had the autumn crisis of 1964 followed *inter alia* by the summer crisis of 1966. It is worth noting in relation to the most recent of our trials that the Chancellor remarked in his budget preview in Parliament on 2 March 1966, that he did not foresee the need for severe increases in taxation, that in his Budget of 3 May 1966, he expected a lull in consumer spending in the months immediately ahead, but by July some of the most drastic economic measures ever undertaken in this country in peacetime had to be introduced by the Prime Minister in person.

Mr Dow has studied the UK economy from 1945 to 1960 with greater thoroughness than anyone else.[1] Two of his many important conclusions are relevant at this stage. On p. 65 he declares:

It is mostly by accident that for most of the time most Chancellors have been successful [and on p. 384 he concludes:] As far as internal conditions are concerned then, budgetary and monetary policy failed to be stabilizing and must on the contrary be regarded as having been positively destabilizing. . . . Had tax changes been more gradual and credit regulations less variable, demand and output would probably have grown much more steadily.

It is true that some reviewers have not been able to accept the latter conclusion but nevertheless one of the more critical still agreed that interventions were excessive.[2]

---

production fell at the rate of 0·5% p.a., it rose at a rate of 9·0% p.a. between 1958 last quarter and 1960 second quarter. Cf. Sir Roy Harrod *Towards a New Economic Policy* (Manchester University Press, Manchester, 1967), pp. 13 and 19.

[1] J. C. R. Dow, *The Management of the British Economy 1945–60* (Cambridge University Press, Cambridge, 1964).

[2] I. M. D. Little, *Economic Journal*, December 1964, p. 983.

It might be added that the conclusion that government policy in the

Why has there been this size of gap between performance and promise? One view on this is to parody the famous lines of Canning and say:

In matters of finance the fault of the British
Is consuming too much and acting too skittish.

But a general statement of this sort does not get us very far. I should be inclined to classify the reasons under two main headings: first, over-simplification of all the issues involved, and second, increasingly ambitious aims over the years.

Over-simplification has many dimensions. At the more theoretical level, one could say that earlier ideas about the stability of the consumption function and hence the investment-income relationship were far too naïve; so also was the notion that there was a single point of equilibrium below which there was less than full employment and beyond which prices started to rise. Nor was anything like adequate allowance made for the pervasive effects of world influences on a highly open economy. Another point is the self-generating character of some economic phenomena: e.g. a low level of unemployment has become a built-in feature of the post-war economy; and when the situation is such that today no one under 40 can remember a period when prices were not rising, is it surprising that economic actions become more and more based on the assumption that this is a permanent state of affairs? Finally, one might point to the theoretical complications of stabilization policy—the danger that government attempts at correction might easily have perverse effects, as shown by the work of Friedman and Phillips.[1]

UK had probably been destabilizing was reached independently by D. J. Smyth, 'Public Finance Policy and Techniques for Economic Stability and Balanced Economic Growth' (International Institute of Public Finance, *Public Finance Policy and Techniques for Economic Stability and Balanced Economic Growth*, Saarbrucken, 1966).

[1] M. Friedman, 'The Effects of a Full-Employment Policy on Economic Stability' (*Essays in Positive Economics*, University of Chicago Press, Chicago, 1953). A. W. Phillips, 'Stabilization Policy in a Closed Economy', *Economic Journal*, June 1954 and 'Stabilization Policy and the Time-Form of Lagged Responses', *Economic Journal*, June 1957.

Many of the more practical difficulties of applying 'the nicely calculated less or more' in the context of macro-economic policy were also underestimated. There have been a number of instances in the post-war years when budgetary policy went badly astray. Dow[1] takes as clear examples the periods 1952–5 and 1958–60. Nearer to the present day, the failure to take action in the summer of 1964 to combat the mounting foreign exchange crisis is another example. The reasons for these failures are manifold. Sometimes the course of events or prospects changed so rapidly that it would have been extremely difficult for any government, however well-equipped and well-intentioned, to have done any better: consider for instance the influence of the Korean War on import prices or the quick deterioration in the balance of payments prospects during the early spring of 1964.[2] There are other cases where one suspects that the forecasting machinery was not as smooth-running as it might have been but with the many improvements in statistical material and techniques one hopes that this will be a diminishing factor in the years to come.[3] Finally, there are some cases where what might be called electoral cost-benefit analysis would appear to have played an important role, e.g. the relaxation of April 1955 in advance of the election of the following month.

Then we have the inability of the government machine to act in a co-ordinated fashion, in such wise that revenue and expenditure policies are reinforcing rather than pulling against one another. If one takes quarterly deseasonalized data of all

[1] *Op. cit.* p. 384. There have, of course, been failures elsewhere as well e.g. errors in 1953, 1954, 1959 and 1962 in the U.S.A. (*Annual Report, Council of Economic Advisers*, Washington, D.C., January 1966, p. 174.)

[2] The 1964 balance of payments on current and long-term capital account was forecast as −£165m in the February issue of the National Institute *Economic Review*; and as −£300m in the May issue.

[3] After explaining that it was very difficult to compare the forecast and actual changes in output between 1958 and 1959 because the actual outcome was still uncertain several years later, Treasury witnesses declared that they considered that statistical deficiences were unlikely to lead to errors in forecasting the domestic economy in future (Fourth Report, Estimates Committee, 1966/67 *Government Statistical Services*, HMSO, London, 1966, paras. 1381–3).

public expenditure on goods and services from 1955–66 (inclusive) and plots the deviations from trend against a measure of the margin of unused resources,[1] one gets the picture shown in the diagram on page 8. The correlation coefficient between the two series is − 0·603.[2]

Obviously, no simple deduction about the perverse influence of government spending policy on the pattern of cycles in the last few years can be drawn from this picture; but at least one can hardly say, when the correlation coefficient is negative and not positive, that public expenditure has followed the pattern one might have expected on simple macro-economic grounds. It would take too long to explore the reasons for all this, but one can say in general that it is extremely difficult to co-ordinate the current or capital expenditure patterns of a highly diversified and multifarious group of authorities;[3] and, more particularly, that very recently we seem to have had a case where local authority spending has been the rogue elephant.[4]

There have also been cases where budgetary policy has not been well co-ordinated with monetary policy. One would like to think that the position had improved over the years since the debacle of the Dalton era. But when it is observed that over the calendar year 1965, a year of alleged retrenchment, the

[1] From F. W. Paish and J. Hennessy, *Policy for Incomes* (Hobart Paper 29, Institute of Economic Affairs, London, Third edition, 1967). I am indebted to Professor Paish for making additional figures available to me.

[2] The time trend fitted to public expenditure was $Y = 1204·7 + 10·68X$ (where Y = public expenditure and X = time). If one fits a time trend to the series for the margin of unused resources, one gets substantially the same results. And the same is true if one measures unused resources by the deseasonalized excess demand for labour data in the *National Institute Review*.

[3] It was stated in *Public Investment in Great Britain* (Cmnd. 1203, HMSO, 1960) that responsibility for investment expenditure was widely diffused with, for instance, 27 gas and electricity boards, 180 local education authorities, 950 government water undertakings, 1,600 sewerage authorities and 1,700 local housing authorities. The result was that it would take 6 months for a decision to change capital expenditure to have significant effects; and 12 for full effects. Although the numbers in some of these categories are less today, the general problem remains.

[4] Cf. Sir John Hicks, *After the Boom* (Institute of Economic Affairs, London, 1966).

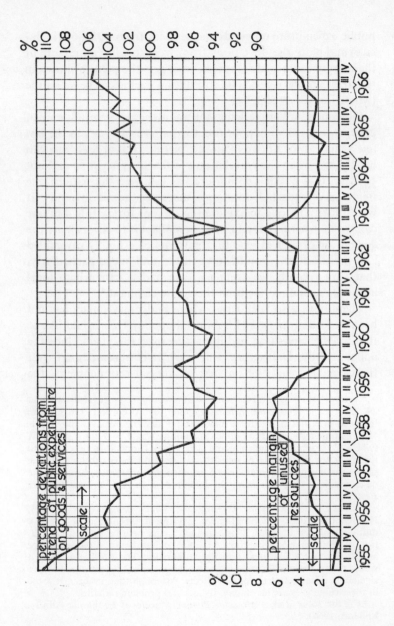

stock of money rose by £915m or some $7\frac{1}{2}\%$,[1] one has some doubts.

Our analysis of the gap between expected and realized results of short-term stabilization measures has so far been cast in terms of over-simplification. We now come to the second major heading: the more ambitious aims of policy-makers over the years. The basic point here is that some of our difficulties have been due to the standards we have set ourselves. The Beveridge Full Employment case was based on the assumption that the *average* employment rate would be 97%; the average rate and the deviations about it have been such that 97% has been just about the *minimum* at any time since the war. Although employment data are not entirely satisfactory as a measure of excess demand, there can be little doubt that if we had chosen to run the economy with 97%, or even $97\frac{1}{2}\%$ average employment instead of something much nearer to $98\frac{1}{2}\%$, we should have had less trouble in the way of cost inflation, imbalance of payments and so on. Although US unemployment data are not directly comparable with UK figures, it is reasonably clear that the US authorities have operated with a lower pressure of demand than in the UK and that difficulties became apparent in 1966 when their position became more like that usually found in the UK.

Another most important sense in which ambitions have grown has been the attempt to fit stabilization policy into a long-term framework. Although there have been many scattered attempts at framing budgetary policy in the context of long-term developments,[2] it is only in recent years that emphasis has been placed on the idea of matching the growth rate of demand with that of supply potential, as given by the forces of population increase, technical progress and so on. This is clearly a much more complex set of aims. First, one has to estimate the growth rate of both demand and supply potential

---

[1] *Financial Statistics* (HMSO, London), March 1967.

[2] In what was possibly the most outstanding budget performance of all time, Gladstone in his 1853 Budget set out a seven-year plan for reducing the income tax to zero; it failed.

with some finesse. Second, circumstances are likely to arise in which short-run considerations dictate a slower or faster rate of growth of demand than long-term ones, with the obvious possibility of output movements diverging from the trend line. Then there is scope for a good deal of argument about the relationships between the pressure of demand and the actual growth rate, e.g. is an employment rate of $98\frac{1}{2}\%$ more conducive to a high growth rate than one of $97\frac{1}{2}\%$ and what is the effect of fluctuations in the pressure of demand on the rate of growth? One also now has to be careful about specifying the appropriate savings ratio: for instance, Harrod-neutral technical improvements would require a constant savings ratio and a rising capital-output ratio would require a rising savings ratio. There are many more complications which we cannot go into here.

To summarize, the conclusion is simply that if one stipulates that policy should be aimed at a very high employment ratio and at the achievement of a growth rate permanently in line with that of productive potential one is pitching one's sights much higher than was common even a few years ago. So it is not surprising that we have experienced a number of setbacks in these endeavours.

What sort of lessons can be drawn, however tentatively, from these experiences? There are certain points on which there is a widespread agreement: for instance, the need for more detailed, more reliable and more up-to-date statistics. On another issue, whether to run the economy at, say, $97\frac{1}{2}\%$ or $98\frac{1}{2}\%$ employment, there is a great deal of disagreement. My own belief is that the former is much more likely to make sense than the latter, but I would not maintain that as yet it has been settled beyond all question. If, for very differing reasons, we leave both these matters on one side, there is still another wide open question about the proper use of budgetary policy. One school of thought is that government should concentrate on a steady rate of growth of demand in line with the long-run growth rate of productive potential. Another is that government should always be ready to take short-term corrective measures, if necessary on a week-by-week, or even a day-by-day, basis. There is obviously some conflict between these two views—though this has not stopped some intellectual acrobats from clinging to both simultaneously!

The former view has, in differing forms and for different reasons, some very distinguished supporters—one of the most recent (albeit in the form of monetary rather than fiscal expansion) being the 1967 US Congressional Joint Economic Committee Report on the President's *Economic Report*. The arguments for this kind of policy are manifold: the importance of generating growth at the full natural rate, the advantages of long-term planning of government expenditure on goods and services on both current and capital account, the political and economic disadvantages of frequent variations in the injection of purchasing power into the economy and so on. On the other hand, we still live in a world where there are substantial short-term changes and these changes are of especial significance for a highly open economy, such as ours. There is also the danger that over a period of time British costs and incomes may gradually move out of alignment with those overseas. There is a variety of ways in which one can try to cope with such disharmonies within the framework of stable long-term government budgetary policies. One is variations in exchange rates; another is a combination of import controls and other internal measures, especially incomes policy; another is to plead for world monetary reform. None of these is free from snags, e.g. the need to maintain at home higher interest rates than abroad if the usual expectation is that sterling will move down; the well-known dangers of import controls; the unlikelihood of sufficient success in the immediate future in securing effective incomes policies or world monetary reform. There is also a further problem. If one goes so far as to argue that government expenditure on goods and services should continue to grow steadily whatever the degree of short-term upset, one is really saying that the burden of any adjustment should fall on the private sector.[1]

[1] This was the (unstated) implication of the argument in favour of

11

This is a particularly important result when, as in the UK, the public sector absorbs a large proportion of GNP.

The second view—the need for 'fine tuning' or continuous government budgetary intervention to adjust aggregate demand —also has many supporters. Some perfectly good reasons exist for this. Short period imbalances can arise rapidly, as we all know only too well; there is no reason why we should be slaves of tradition in budgetary procedure, insisting on one (or perhaps two) major series of changes per annum and at preordained times of the year. Policy on such lines is also feasible. Even though one cannot always engineer quick changes in government spending,[1] there are ways in which tax rates can be varied quickly in this country—in marked contrast to the USA.

Equally clearly, there are objections to this type of policy. There is a major constitutional problem: it may not always be easy to fit quick changes into the parliamentary legislative programme and, if it is not, how much discretion is it right and proper to give to the executive in such matters? Also, greater frequency of intervention may do more to destabilize than to stabilize, in so far as incorrect predictions are made, lags insufficiently allowed for, and so on. During the period October 1964–July 1966 the number of 'mini-Budgets' was so great that more or less the only way of keeping up with them was constant perusal of all economic intelligence—in much the same way as Horace Walpole is alleged to have said in the *Annus Mirabilis* of 1759 that he had to enquire every day whether there had been another victory, in case he missed one. Nevertheless, it was still necessary to supplement all these measures with the severe deflationary package of 20 July 1966: the very kind of intervention that constant small adjustments are supposed to obviate.

---

stability of government programmes in the Plowden Committee Report, cf. *Report of Committee in Control of Public Expenditure*, Cmnd. 1432, HMSO, London, 1961.

[1] For technical and organizational reasons in the case of goods and services; for institutional reasons in the case of transfer payments.

Finally, it is not clear how businessmen react to frequent small-scale changes rather than infrequent larger ones. Are they more likely to go ahead with plans for expansion, or installation of new equipment if they never know where they are than if they only have to face occasional changes, even though the latter may be on a larger scale?

My own preference is for a policy intermediate between these views: i.e. one which tries to ensure a reasonably adequate long-term growth of demand without completely sacrificing short-term adaptability. It should not be thought that this is easy. To illustrate, take the question of the built-in flexibility of taxation. Short-term domestic fluctuations are likely[1] to be eased the more the revenue structure has this characteristic; but externally led fluctuations raise further issues. Then over the long run, revenue buoyancy may be embarrassing and the economy become subject to 'fiscal drag', if conditions are of the US type; but if public expenditure threatens to forge ahead, as appears to be the prospect in the UK in the next few years, revenue buoyancy is needed to hold down the rate of growth of private demand. Despite these and other complications, one would hope that a reasonable degree of built-in flexibility would cut down the need for frequent short-run tax-rate changes. If there were also an extension of Regulator powers, whereby the executive is permitted to make strictly circumscribed adjustments to tax rates without prior reference to Parliament,[2] one should then be able to secure a reasonable degree of short-term adjustment without losing sight of longer term changes.

Prescriptions of this sort are inevitably subject to the charge that they are no more than commonsense. But in a field where, more often than not, the modern version of Gresham's law prevails ('wishful political thinking drives out economic commonsense'), this may be no bad thing.

[1] *Not* certainly. Cf. D. J. Smyth, 'Can Automatic Stabilizers be De-Stabilizing?', *Public Finance*, IV, 1963.

[2] I should, incidentally, say that my own preference is for the Regulator in its original (1961) form when all the relevant rates had to be changed in the same proportion rather than the new (1964) form which allows for greater discretion.

II

Our next concern is budgetary investment stimuli. The history of these in the post-war period is complicated, with the mixture of initial allowances, investment allowances, free depreciation and investment grants, but sufficiently well known in outline not to need repetition. Instead, we shall concentrate on three questions:

(1) The effectiveness of such devices in stimulating investment.

(2) The effects of stimulating investment on the level and growth rate of GNP.

(3) A possible alternative policy.

(1) Evidence is mixed on this. On the one hand, one can point to the fact that by and large investment stimuli have become more generous over the post-war period and that the gross investment/GNP ratio has also risen. And in particular one can single out the investment boom of 1955 and argue, with some show of reasonableness, that this was not unconnected with the introduction of investment allowances in 1954. On the other hand, a variety of enquiries conducted in recent years[1] among businessmen seemed to suggest that initial and investment allowances had very little influence on decisions to invest. It is too early to say whether the response to the new investment grants is likely to be different but unless and until there is some positive evidence that it is—and such evidence may be extremely hard to establish for the current period in view of the simultaneous changes in other likely determinants of investment— one must remain sceptical about the magnitude of any change in attitudes.

It is easy to pick holes in both views. On the first, one can say that it is hard to distinguish cause and effect and to isolate the

[1] See, e.g., *Report of Committee on Turnover Taxation*, Cmnd. 2300 (HMSO, 1964); R. R. Neild, 'Replacement Policy', *National Institute Review*, November 1964; D. C. Corner and Alan Williams, 'The Sensitivity of Businesses to Initial and Investment Allowances', *Economica*, February 1965; NEDC, *Investment in Machine Tools* (HMSO, 1965).

influence of these measures on the higher level of investment. On the second, there are all the old problems of businessmen rationalizing answers to such questions. The most likely answer in our present state of knowledge is that such stimuli have a minor but not a major effect on the level of investment and the ratio of investment to GNP.

(2) The effects of investment on the level of GNP and its rate of growth is the subject of an enormous volume of literature, both at theoretical and applied levels. Confining ourselves entirely to the latter, one can again find conflicting evidence. For instance, Sir Robert Shone[1] has argued as if there is a causal connection between the facts that the investment ratio rose from 14% in 1947–52 to 19% in 1964, and that productivity rose substantially over the same period. On the other hand, more extensive investigations of these matters have not found a very substantial connection. For instance, Professor Matthews[2] found that from 1948–62 the average annual percentage increase in GDP per man-year was 1·9% but only 0·6% could be explained by changes in capital per man, leaving a residual factor of 1·3%.[3] Other studies, both of this country, and of others, have come out with similar sorts of conclusions.[4]

There is obviously a great deal more to be done in this field (e.g. the further development of the vintage approach pioneered by Salter and Solow[5]) and it would be the height of foolishness to proclaim that we are anywhere in sight of certainty in such

[1] Sir R. Shone, *Investment and Economic Growth* (University of London, Athlone Press, 1966), p. 7.
[2] R. C. O. Matthews, 'Some Aspects of Post-War Growth in the British Economy in Relation to Historical Experience', *Transactions of Manchester Statistical Society*, 1964–5, p. 3.
[3] It should be added that this residual factor was absolutely higher in the post-war period than in the pre-war one but lower relatively to the capital factor.
[4] Cf. W. Beckerman *et al.*, *The British Economy in 1975* (Cambridge University Press, Cambridge, 1965), p. 41.
[5] See, e.g., W. E. G. Salter, *Productivity and Technical Change* (Cambridge University Press, Cambridge, 1960); and R. M. Solow, *Capital Theory and the Rate of Return* (North Holland, Amsterdam, 1963).

studies. At the same time, it does look as if some of the earlier notions that all that one needed to do to push an economy along faster was to raise the investment ratio were far too *simpliste*. It may be that we shall in the end find that there are one or two simple things—whether in some form of capital investment or another easily distinguished element of input—which reveal all the secrets. But may it not also be that such quests are as fruitless as those for the philosopher's stone or the secrets of longevity? Time may, or may not, tell.

(3) If, in the meantime, we must accept as a working hypothesis that the connections between investment stimuli and investment and those between investment and the growth rate are unclear, it may be that there is a case for reconsidering the ways in which budgetary measures can be used to help in the growth process. Of course, there is no shortage of suggestions for suitable measures; maintenance of a steady growth of demand in line with the growth of productive potential; measures to push exports; technology; education; training; and so on *ad infinitum*. What I fear, however, is that if the growth process is so subtle and complex, we may well find ourselves in a continuing situation whereby we prostrate ourselves to one of these new gods for a time, then discover—no doubt, after suitably large expenditure of public funds—that it does not hold the keys to the promised land, and reject it for another one—and so on.

It may be preferable to seek a more direct line of approach. Like most ideas in economics, this is not a new one. Indeed, claims to originality in such matters are much more frequently a sign of inadequate reading of the literature than of anything else. In 1961, Professor K. Knorr and W. J. Baumol edited a book[1] in which the idea was mooted that an appropriate fiscal stimulant would be to grant a rebate to firms on the basis of their additions to value added between one year and the next. Although Professor Baumol would apparently now like to

[1] *What Price Economic Growth?* (Prentice Hall, Englewood Cliffs, New Jersey, 1961).

modify his original proposals,[1] my own view is that they do still contain a great deal of merit.

The fundamental point is that one is then tackling the problem directly by giving larger fiscal rewards to those firms which register larger increases in output—a kind of payment by results scheme on a large scale. If a major policy aim is to encourage output growth and if we are uncertain about the relative strengths of the many reasons for output growth, surely it may make better sense to approach it in this direct fashion, rather than making one grant here for investment in physical capital, another there for expenditure on research and another there for retraining labour, and so on.

Needless to say, there are many detailed problems. It would obviously be much easier to operate a scheme of this sort if one already had a value-added tax in existence. But there are clearly a number of reasons for thinking that this is a possible development in any case. Then there would be difficulties about the basis of calculating value added. Whereas, for tax purposes, it is usually accepted that the most appropriate computation is one which excludes capital investment expenditure, the more relevant basis for rebate or subsidy would be the annual differences in gross value added, before deducting capital expenditure. Otherwise increments in value added, and hence rebates, would *pro tanto* be smaller the greater the investment spending in a period. Whilst one may have doubts about the strength and nature of the influence of investment on output growth, there is certainly no need to go to the other extreme and penalize investment.

One point which troubled the authors in the original exposition[2] was the need to correct additions to value added for price changes. In so far as these are due to general changes in the price level, my worries would not be so great: the fact that a government knows that the rebates to be granted will be greater, the more it allows inflation to develop, might even make for less official complacency about prices. In so far as

[1] Cf. 'A Possible Tax Stimulus for Productivity', *Financial Times*, 4 August 1966.　　[2] *What Price Economic Growth?* p. 36.

the price changes are due to exercising a monopoly position, the position is more difficult but even here it might be a once-for-all process (if exploiting previously neglected opportunities) or a sign of weakness of other policies (if successive increases in monopoly power over the years go unchecked).

Many other problems arise. One might be called on to square a policy of this sort with one of succouring declining industries or regions; if so, differential excise or payroll taxes could do a good deal, though this raises further complications, as we shall see later. If one works on the principle that rebates are given for increases in value added but that the process is asymmetrical (i.e. no additional liabilities are incurred if there is a fall in value added), one may then have considerable differences in treatment between firms with highly fluctuating records and those with records of steady growth. For instance, if two firms had the same increment in value added over a five-year period but one achieved it by a succession of decrements and large increments and the other by a succession of small increments, the former would get a larger rebate over the whole period. However, if the fluctuations in output are a reflection of greater risks undertaken, this may not be a bad result. There are also further problems of newborn and dying firms to be thought about, but we should overrun our space if we tried to go into them here.

No doubt, many other points arise in such a complicated change. But I would strongly argue that a direct approach of this sort should certainly not be ruled out, except after most searching and far-reaching enquiries.

III

We have said something about lessons to be learned from the attempts to keep aggregate demand and supply balanced and the attempts to stimulate growth through investment. We now pass to a field which is both wider and narrower—wider in the sense that there have been a large number of measures or non-measures relatively unconnected with one another and yet narrower in the sense that rather more limited objectives have usually been in mind.

There are clearly problems of definition (e.g. what do we mean by neutrality, non-discrimination, etc.?) when discussing the range and size of specific government subsidies, tax remissions, etc., for particular purposes. Rather than take up time by attempting to make precise definitions—and probably not succeeding—we shall try to indicate by a number of examples the sorts of considerations in mind.

One might start by quoting the answers given in Parliament to questions about recent changes in subsidies, grants, etc.[1] However, broad answers of this sort do not get us very far and we can probably do better by singling out some of the more obvious cases, even if this does involve the risk of bias in selection. One particular field is road transport. Many people have argued the case for a congestion tax[2] in city centres and we need not repeat the arguments here. So far, although there have been promises of further study at official levels, that seems to be about all. But among the consequences of the present implicit subsidy to city vehicle users are the increasingly obvious difficulties of public urban transport—buses are held up because of road congestion, fares are raised to try to cover costs, more people turn to private transport, further financial difficulties arise—leading eventually to substantial subsidies to public transport. This is a clear case of one form of 'subsidy' breeding another one with the consequences of overall cheapening of passenger transport, encouragement of commuting and so on.

In the case of the coal industry, there has been a variety of means of protection—bans on imports, the tax on heavy fuel oil and 'persuasion' of the electricity industry to build coal-

[1] See e.g. Hansard (Commons) 10 March 1966, cols. 658–60, and 23 March 1967, cols. 354–8.

[2] Cf. *Road Pricing: The Economic and Technical Possibilities* (Ministry of Transport, London, 1964); A. A. Walters 'The Theory and Measurement of Private and Social Costs of Congestion', *Econometrica*, October 1961; G. J. Roth, *A Self-Financing Road System* (Institute of Economic Affairs, London, 1966); and *Better Use of Town Roads* (HMSO, London, June 1967).

fired power stations. The validity of the arguments for coal protection might in turn provoke less scepticism if we did not hear the exact opposite of the declining industry argument in other cases, e.g. computers. If, as a matter of general principle, government help is needed both for declining and for growing industries, how much is left which does not need help?

In the last year or so, policy differentiation has taken another form. The restriction of investment grants to manufacturing and extractive industry, the introduction of Selective Employment Tax with its differential refunds and more recently the proposals to introduce still further differentiation in the repayments to manufacturing industry in Development Areas[1] are all of a pattern. It is perhaps not entirely fortuitous that an intellectual argument for such provisions is to be found in Professor Kaldor's inaugural lecture at Cambridge.[2] Whatever the merits of the arguments about increasing returns and learning by doing in the manufacturing sector, it can hardly be contended that all the consequences of the new system were fully foreseen. The need to consider new help to Development Areas; the report in March 1967 of the NEDC 'little Neddy' on distribution; and the 1967 changes in respect of part-time workers are sufficient evidence. And some of the more bizarre results, such as the tribulations of local authorities[3] or the argument[4] that the Area Electricity Boards (not subject to tax) should raise the prices they quote for contract work when in competition with private contractors (subject to tax) at a time when there was an official price freeze policy have to be spelled out to be believed.

A great deal could be said about regional policy. First, there are a number of ministries involved in important ways, e.g.

[1] *The Development Areas: a Proposal for a Regional Employment Premium* (HMSO, April 1967); and *The Development Areas: Regional Employment Premiums* (HMSO, June 1967). A welcome should be given to the open invitation to advance discussion of this proposal.

[2] *Causes of the Slow Rate of Economic Growth of the UK* (Cambridge University Press, Cambridge, 1966).

[3] See H. R. Page, 'Sense and Nonsense', *Local Government Finance*, December 1966.

[4] See *The Guardian*, 11 October 1966.

the Department of Economic Affairs, the Board of Trade and (through both control over physical planning and the system of grants to local authorities) the Ministry of Housing and Local Government. Their policies have changed frequently in recent years and it is by no means clear that they have always been closely co-ordinated, to put it mildly. We have a variety of different subsidies, some of which are certainly pulling against one another. How far, for instance, would the pull of London be reduced, and the regional need for grants etc. be alleviated if Londoners did not receive transport subsidies? And, although one can see some arguments in favour of the recent proposals for additional SET refunds in the Development Areas, the fact remains that with one measure (investment grants) one is encouraging capital-intensive industries or methods and with the other (SET refunds) one is encouraging labour-intensive industries or methods. It is difficult to believe that such a combination is appropriate for the whole of manufacturing industry (but no other industries) in the whole of the Development Areas (but no other areas).

Turning to general policy on income distribution one can find a very similar state of affairs. Merrett and Monk[1] have recently argued that a large part of the redistributive side of taxation (as distinct from transfer payments) in this country is more apparent than real and that the 1962/3 tax system (other than company taxes, death duties and surtax) could have been replaced by a uniform sales tax of about 28% without any important distributional consequences between income groups. Although I have reservations about these particular calculations and about the suggested alternative,[2] the proposition that a lot

[1] A. J. Merrett and D. A. G. Monk, 'The Structure of UK Taxation 1962/3', *Oxford Bulletin of Statistics*, August 1966.

[2] There is surely a great deal to be said for ensuring that a substantial part of the total tax burden is placed on individuals in the form of direct taxation. The more one moves away to a system where nobody knows what he is paying or even that he is paying, the less interest the average citizen is likely to take in the role and scope of government spending. Hence the more likely it is that this will expand without let or hindrance. A rise in personal income tax comes home to the individual much more than a rise in value-added tax or corporation tax. It is the progression

21

of the alleged redistributional effects of taxation are mythical takes a lot of controverting.

More specific measures in the income redistribution field are legion but let us take housing as an example. The final elimination of Schedule A tax for owner-occupiers in 1963 was greeted with loud applause. Now it has been realized that this opened a Pandora's box, in that by leaving the whole of any mortgage interest payments by an owner-occupier to be claimed as a deduction against ordinary income, the effective cost of such housing is now less the higher the individual's tax rate. Therefore legislation has now been introduced to give hand-outs in the form of option mortgages to those paying tax at low or zero rates. As another example from the housing field, we have the report that in one Scottish city tenants occupying low-rented municipally provided houses object to paying realistic rents for garages on the grounds that garage rents might then be higher than house rents; but if one cannot charge realistic rents for garages, how can one charge realistic prices for parking in city streets—and so on?

As another example, take the argument about large families. Simultaneously, there seem to be signs of official moves in 1967 to reform the Family Allowance system so as to give more help to larger families and at the same time to subsidize birth control measures. If extra support for larger families were limited to those already in being, there would be no conflict; but as it is, the government is open to the charge that it is simultaneously encouraging larger and smaller families.

As a last example, I cannot refrain from reproducing a passage from *The Guardian* of 25 April 1967. Although it is not a matter of revenue and expenditure policy, and so really falls outside the scope of this paper, it is such a perfect example of the dangers of trying to govern in excessive detail that it simply

---

rather than the principle of direct taxation which is at fault. For analogous reasons, I am not at all persuaded of the desirability of the recent legislation to shift part of the burden of local rates away from the domestic ratepayer.

must be recorded. I reproduce the passage more or less in full; comment is totally superfluous.

Joanna Wilkinson, aged 9, of Nottingham complained to her M.P. when the cost of a packet of marbles at the local shop went up by a penny to sevenpence. Mr. Michael English (Labour, Nottingham West) took up the matter with the Board of Trade and after a full investigation Joanna has had her penny refunded and the cost of marbles has been adjusted. Joanna . . . told her M.P. that she thought sixpence was enough to pay for a packet of marbles. Mr. English found that the shopkeeper was only passing on to her a price increase he had to pay when buying the marbles.

Surely some lessons can be learned from this small sample of examples, culled from a large population. The main conclusion is analogous to one made above: in just the same way that it is far from clear that increased frequency of government intervention assures stability of the economy, so it is very possible that an increasingly complex pattern of subsidies, tax reliefs and so on is self-defeating, whether in defending one industry, one region or one person against another. There are clearly some cases where a second measure has to be taken to make sure that the first is effective, but at least as often the second step may, by design or accident, offset the first one. If the first step was misguided the self-cancellation process may be desirable anyway; but it would be even more desirable to have neither measure.

Another point is surely that one must be very inquisitive about the precise reasons for steps of this kind. Vague phrases such as 'the public interest' and 'social priorities' are meaningless as they stand; and given a tiny bit of ingenuity, well within the bounds of any industrial or regional spokesmen, external economies or growth arguments can always be made to sound convincing, whatever the context.

One must also beware of the dangers that arise through unnecessary splitting of functions between departments. We noticed the danger in connection with regional policy. The same phenomenon has also arisen in recent years with investment stimuli (investment grants through the Board of Trade, and initial allowances through the Inland Revenue) and with SET refunds (responsibility being shared between the Ministry of Labour, the Ministry of Social Security and the Ministry of Agriculture). Such fragmentation is bound to lead to lack of co-ordination as well as to additional administration costs.[1]

More generally, the older role of Parliament was to protect the taxpayer against the Crown, or executive. A little more attention to this role today would surely not come amiss. For there is little sign that the executive itself is distinguished by its capacity for learning by misdoing.

IV

How can I possibly summarize this long and wide-ranging address without being even more superficial? Clearly I must try, whatever the risks.

By and large, one must conclude that our record with revenue and expenditure policy has not been a particularly glorious one in the last twenty years. Whether one looks at the succession of stop-go crises, the growth history or the series of *ad hoc* devices to shore up particular interests we have a mixed record. It is worth noting, *en passant*, that the old argument that our budgetary problems are so much worse than our predecessors' because of the pace of scientific advance, technological change, etc., is far from convincing. To take one example, Mr Robert Blake points out, in his biography of Disraeli,[2] that when Disraeli was Chancellor for the second time in 1858 he was faced with all the financial implications of a complete revolution in naval requirements in that simultaneously wooden ships had to be replaced by iron, armour plating was added, and the screw and steam came into use. Nevertheless, he and his successors managed.

[1] One great attraction of the proposals for a negative income tax, currently under intensive discussion in the USA, is that they are a means of integrating social security payments with the income tax machinery, thereby eliminating, rather than increasing, duplication between government departments.

[2] R. Blake, *Disraeli* (Eyre and Spottiswoode, London, 1966), p. 398.

More rewarding than an analysis of all the reasons for our mixed record is one of where economists in particular have been at fault. Surely there can be no question that many have been too ambitious. On far too many occasions, policies have been advocated on the basis of untested, or insufficiently tested, hypotheses and a far too casual acquaintance with the facts. Statistical limitations and deficiencies have too often been minimized or ignored in the anxiety to advocate some new gimmick. And consultations with industrialists and others with their feet on the ground have been much less frequent than they ought to have been. One hopes that some of these lessons may have been learned from recent events. But if the professional reputation of economists is not to be further tarnished there is another point of major importance: one role of the economist is surely to resist at all times the idea that one can disguise weak policies by jargon, claptrap or pretentious names or that one should accept a programme containing weak policies as a means of securing acceptance of some strong ones. Abnegation of professional standards for political purposes is the surest way to self-destruction.

I began this presidential address by referring to that by Alfred Marshall in 1890. I end with a quotation from that extraordinarily sagacious man:

Every statement in regard to economic affairs which is short is a misleading fragment, a fallacy or a truism. I think this dictum of mine is an exception to the general rule: but I am not bold enough to say that it *certainly* is.[1]

I leave it to others to decide whether my discussion has or has not escaped these traps.

[1] A. C. Pigou (ed.), *Memorials of Alfred Marshall* (Macmillan, 1925), p. 484.

2

F A Cockfield

Central government taxation

I start from the point of view that prima facie all taxes are bad. They are bad because they distort the economy: they are bad because they depress initiative and enterprise and they are bad because they replace individual choice by choice of government.

It is necessary to make this declaration of principle, right at the start because it is directly contrary to the view commonly acted upon. Taxation and its concomitant government expenditure are the great growth industry of our time: unfortunately today they are our only growth industry.

I believe that fundamentally we suffer from too much taxation. Thirty-three per cent of everything we produce or earn now passes through the hands of the central government in taxation: and if we add local government taxation the figure is much higher. There has recently been an attempt to try and show that the position is not as bad as I have indicated and this argument has been supported by quoting figures for government expenditure on goods and services. This of course is much less than total government expenditure. This approach is correct if one is looking at the proportion of economic resources absorbed by government. But it is quite wrong if what one is concerned about is the level of taxation. From this point of view what matters is the total amount of tax raised: it is quite beside the point whether the government then spends the money on goods and services or disburses it in transfer payments.

There is nothing inevitable about the present level of taxation, except that it is the inevitable result of the present level of government expenditure. This in turn flows from a mistaken view of the proper relationship between the individual and the state. It is a reflection of the view that the state is the supreme father figure and that it is the duty of the state to provide and of the individual to receive. This philosophy I entirely reject. The fundamental unit of society is the individual and the family: the role of the state should be limited to the provision of the services the individual cannot provide himself.

I realize that any comment on the level of government expenditure leads to a demand that one should specify the services on which economies should be made. I do not think this is a valid argument. If the government were prepared to take a smaller proportion of the national product and leave a larger proportion available for investment and exports, the rate of growth of the economy would be higher than it is at present and out of this higher level of production we should ultimately be able to afford more and not less for welfare and other desirable services.

Government expenditure as such lies outside my field of discussion and I mention it as indeed I must because it is the level of government expenditure which lies at the root of the present level of taxation and all the damage that this does.

The Labour Party came to power in 1964 with great reforming zeal. But what has emerged in the field of taxation has not been reform based on solid principle but a series of doctrinal changes which have altered the whole fabric of our tax system with few advantages and many disadvantages. This has been completed with heavy increases in the level of taxation, some overt, others covert. We have ended up therefore with the worst of both worlds: bad taxes and heavy taxes. What we really want are good taxes and light taxes.

I propose to start by looking at the basic principles on which taxation ought to rest.

I do not quarrel with the broad view that the government has responsibility for the general management of the economy and that the level of taxation is one of the weapons at its disposal. But even here I would enter a number of caveats. Wise government could often avoid getting into the situation where taxation has had to be used as a weapon. Secondly, the interplay of expenditure and taxation often produces extremely undesirable results. During a recession government expenditure is permitted to rise, or even provoked to rise, to stimulate the economy. In due course, when the private sector of the economy picks up, the rise in public expenditure, plus the rise in private expenditure, overloads the economy. Taxes are then increased as a counter-inflationary measure. We end up therefore with government expenditure and taxes chasing one another upwards in a vicious spiral.

The size of tax variations which need to be made for countercyclical reasons is comparatively small. Total tax revenue now exceeds £10,000m per annum. Changes in the level of taxation for economic reasons rarely amount to much more than £100m to £200m. This is very much a question of the tail wagging the dog. We ought not to allow our thoughts to be dominated by this question of economic management: it is a legitimate use of taxation but a minor one and our tax system ought to rest on a much more fundamental basis of philosophy.

The first clear attempt to use taxation to achieve specific economic ends lay in the introduction of initial allowances in the Income Tax Act of 1945, the last fiscal act of the wartime coalition government. Since then the proliferation of these devices has been endless. Initial allowances, investment allowances and now investment grants: manipulation of purchase tax rates: free depreciation for plant in development regions: special treatment for specific types of expenditure, such as ships, research or computers: differential rates of profits tax: the corporation tax: and now the SET.

I have two basic objections to all this. First of all, the inducements or penalties are rarely effective, they frequently work in the wrong direction and are often based on theoretic arguments remote from the practical everyday world. Some of the arguments advanced are so fatuous that the kindest comment that can be made is that they have been thought up after the event to justify something which had already been decided.

28

Many of these devices have been modified or abandoned: in particular the frequent manipulation of rates of initial or investment allowances and of purchase tax. But the SET with its absurd pretentions to remodel the economy in a dozen different ways shows that the old Adam is still there. Essentially this approach to taxation is based on an assumption that we can do much more than we can in fact do: that we are masters of a situation that we are not masters of. We would be better advised to take a more humble approach.

My second objection is that all these devices mean that the general level of taxation is much higher than it needs to be. This is bad psychologically and it also means that the person who is not the fortunate recipient of one of these favours has to pay a great deal more than he otherwise would have to do.

My own approach to the economic uses of taxation is a very simple one. We ought to recognize that our wisdom and our powers are limited. We cannot achieve the vast effects that it is so easy to talk about. Our endeavours ought to be directed to the more modest aim of ensuring that the taxes we do impose do as little harm as possible.

The primary purpose of taxation is to share the cost of common services among the members of the community as fairly as possible. Of course, people's views of fairness will differ. But unfortunately in recent years the concept of fairness to the individual or to the taxpayer has been brushed to one side in a determination to pursue economic and political theories. Corporation tax is a prime example of this. The changes in liability, and many of them were very big, as between one company and another and as between one class of capital and another, had no foundation in equity. In some instances they were defended on grounds of political theory but very often were little more than the inevitable and often unforeseen by-product of the determination to adopt a particular form of company taxation. SET is an even more extreme example with its attempt to divide the citizens of this country into two groups—the sheep and goats, the productive and the unproductive. For a party which has throughout its history denounced social injustice this introduction of the caste system into taxation policy is a shameful thing.

One's views of the sort of tax system one wants must therefore emerge from one's views of social policy. Briefly I would define the system we need as one which should be based primarily on a fair distribution of the cost of common services; which should produce as few distortions in the economy as possible; which should eschew economic gimmickry; and which should be as simple as possible.

It may be thought surprising in view of what I have said that I should choose as my principal target Income Tax which has long been regarded as the fairest of taxes. But there is a vast difference between fairness as a theoretical concept and what actually emerges in practice. It is true that income tax (including the surtax) can be graduated by reference to the size of income: can be imposed at different rates on earned and investment income and adjusted to take account of family responsibilities and other special circumstances. But when one comes to examine these facets of the tax its claim to supreme fairness as a taxing instrument begins to evaporate. While it may be admitted that the bigger incomes should pay higher rates of tax than the smaller incomes, the steepness of the graduation must be a matter of subjective judgment: there can be no objective standard. Many people would regard the current rates of tax as being far removed from any concept of fairness or equity and tantamount at the top, where they reach $96\frac{1}{4}\%$, to confiscation.

Even more intriguing is the concept that the higher rates of tax charged on investment income represent in some way a special kind of equity embodied in the income tax. No one has ever advanced a satisfactory, let alone a unanimously held explanation of this feature in the tax. When Lloyd George first introduced the differentiation against investment income he said that the reasons were so obvious they needed no exposition; which is simply another way of saying that there weren't any logical reasons, the measure being based on pure prejudice. Since Lloyd George's day there have been many

30

attempts at *post hoc* rationalization of the situation. The best explanation which can be advanced is that investment income is backed by capital and can therefore legitimately be expected to pay more. But this reasoning, if accepted, might be a reason for taxing the capital: it is no particular justification for taxing the income.

The third argument advanced in favour of the income tax, namely that it allows regard to be paid to differing family circumstances, is itself the subject of much contention as every Finance Bill debate shows. There may be a principle of fairness somewhere here, but no two people will ever agree on what the measure should be. The latest development in this particular field is seen in the claim that the income tax child allowances should actually be abolished on the argument that they are unfair to the non-income tax payer and the money should be distributed to everyone, taxpayers and non-taxpayers, in the form of higher cash family allowances.

The claim to unique fairness advanced on behalf of the income tax cannot be substantiated; but this does not mean that the income tax is a bad tax. Nor indeed does the fact that the tax damages incentive and places a penalty on enterprise mean that it is necessarily a bad tax. What has happened is that the tax has been pushed too far and it has been expected to shoulder too big a share of the total burden of government expenditure. It is this which has led to the excessive rates and evil economic effects to which I have referred and it is this which has exacerbated the imperfections of the tax. I believe that our major task today is to topple the income tax from the pinnacle of pre-eminence which it has occupied for so long. If we reduce the income tax to a smaller tax, imposed at more modest rates, we can turn it once more into a reasonable tax, a well-accepted tax and a less damaging tax.

If one is to make sensible changes in income tax, and indeed in other taxes as well, it cannot be done except at considerable cost. This means that we must find some major source of revenue elsewhere. It is in this context that value-added tax is well worth re-examination.

My own view is that the Richardson Committee were asked the wrong question and not surprisingly therefore gave the wrong answer.

What has gone wrong with the argument over value-added tax is that its advocates have argued as if it were really a special kind of income tax or profits tax, charged not on the surplus of receipts over all expenses but the surplus of receipts over certain specified expenses, viz. the cost of materials, depreciation, etc. They have said or implied that it would be assessed and collected once a year like the income tax and on this basis they have tried to argue that it would not necessarily be passed on in prices; and indeed would not be passed on if when the tax was imposed there was a corresponding reduction in profits tax (or corporation tax as it would now be).

I think the whole of this argument is quite misleading. The value-added tax in France and as contemplated in the other countries of the EEC is very clearly an indirect tax imposed on goods and services: it appears as such on all invoices: and is collected monthly on the basis of tax invoiced and not on an annual income tax style computation.

This view of the true nature of value-added tax is supported by GATT: the reason why value-added tax is rebateable on exports is that it is genuinely an indirect tax, not a cleverly disguised direct tax.

The people who advocate value-added tax on what I would describe as the 'modified income tax' basis do themselves a great disservice because their arguments both as to the nature and effect of the tax can so easily be shown to be wrong.

We can only come to a correct judgment about value-added tax if we start by recognizing its true nature, viz. that it is a widely based indirect tax; and recognizing its true effect, namely that it is going to be passed on in prices.

Once we reach this point we are in a proper position to assess the correctness of the Richardson Committee's conclusion. In my opinion the conclusion reached by the Richardson Committee is wrong. It is wrong because, as I have already indicated, they were asked the wrong question; as indeed in

1963 when the Committee was appointed everyone (including myself) was asking the wrong question. As this point is of great importance I propose pursuing it in detail.

The Richardson Committee were asked to consider 'the introduction in this country (as a possible substitute for the purchase tax or the profits tax) of . . . a value-added tax'. These words are from the Chancellor's Budget speech. Admittedly in the actual terms of reference the words 'either in addition to existing taxation, or . . .' were slipped in. But the Richardson Committee dismissed this piece of Treasury cupidity very curtly: 'We took it that our terms of reference . . . did not require this.'

I suggest that the substitution of a value-added tax for the purchase tax or the profits tax (or a tranche of the corporation tax) is not the real point in issue. What we want is a new widely based tax which would provide the broad substratum of a new tax system, a tax which might yield say £2,000m gross or £1,000m net. There is a good chance that the value-added tax could fulfil this role. Of course if it did the purchase tax would disappear, but this is merely a consequential effect. The real purpose of the change is not the substitution of one tax for another but the provision of a massive new source of revenue in an acceptable form which would permit us to undertake a reconstruction of our existing tax system.

The revenue to be obtained from a value-added tax will depend on its coverage and the rates at which it is imposed. But it is worth bearing in mind that when the Richardson Committee reported some years ago the French value-added tax even then yielded over £2,000m and the yield is now probably nearer £3,000m. On this basis and allowing for the disappearance of the purchase tax and compensating adjustments in the rates of the taxes on tobacco, alcohol and petrol it is clear that there is a major source of new revenue here. It is not my objective today to try and quantify these matters in precise form but to suggest general lines of policy. If after all the consequential effects had been taken into account we were left with a net additional revenue equal to one half of the yield of the tax in France this is clearly enough to enable us to undertake a major reconstruction of the present tax system as well as to improve welfare benefits to compensate particular groups of people who may suffer unduly from the change; and even to give positive help for example to people with large families.

Nor do I propose going into any great detail as to the precise nature of the changes in the existing system which should be financed out of the additional revenue accruing from the value-added tax. Clearly the prime candidate here is the income tax and surtax. They are of course really two parts of a single tax, as indeed in law they are. The present graduation is quite absurd both at the bottom as well as at the top. The tax rates rise very steeply on the first few hundred pounds of taxable income; there is then a long band up to about £5,000 a year taxed at the standard rate; and the rates then rise rapidly again to a maximum of well over 90%. We obviously need a new graduation more moderate at the bottom, smoother in the middle and rising to a maximum comparable to the 70% charged in the United States. At the same time it would be a major simplification if the additional charge levied on investment income could be taken out of income tax altogether. I have already referred to the fact that we tax capital very heavily elsewhere—mainly through estate duty. The cost of removing the differential against investment income has been quoted as £200m. If it were felt that this was too much and represented a disproportionate share of the new revenue available, part of the cost at any rate could be recouped by closing the loopholes in estate duty and imposing a tax on gifts. It is perhaps worth mentioning that for the last year for which figures have been published, voluntary dispositions amounted to £185m. This is by no means the total amount of gifts, many if not most of which are made primarily to avoid estate duty. The revenue which could be recouped by taxing these gifts would clearly be substantial.

There is an enormous psychological gain which can be made once the discrimination against investment income is removed from the income tax. Once this is done all income whether earned or investment would be charged at the same rate. This would enable us to merge the earned income relief into the tax rates and thus make very big reductions in the nominal rates of tax. The present standard rate of 8s. 3d. in the £ is equal to an effective rate of 6s. 5d. If as part of the general reduction in the rates of direct taxation the income tax rates were reduced by 6d., this could produce a net standard rate on the new system of 6s. The psychological benefits of having a rate as low as this would be very great. The income tax at present suffers a great deal from appearing to be much worse than it is: it is bad enough but it looks even worse.

No one would pretend that the changes I have mentioned would be anything other than very costly. A 6d. reduction in all rates of income tax costs more than £200m: the removal of the investment income differential costs another £200m. If we earmark a further £200m for improvements in the graduation itself this makes a total of £600m or so. But if value-added tax yielded net £1,000m, and it would probably yield more than this, this still leaves a very big sum indeed for improved welfare payments and other tax changes.

It will no doubt be argued that a programme of this kind by reducing the taxes on income and increasing the taxes on goods and services is unfair to the poorer sections of the community. This is not so. There are now nearly 20 million people paying income tax and with their families they represent the greater part of the total population. The income tax changes are weighted at the bottom of the scale: a reduction of 6d. in the reduced rates is a much bigger proportion of the tax bill than a reduction of 6d. in the standard rate. Secondly the impact of the changes on the really needy can effectively be countered by welfare payments for which ample finance would be available. The effect of the proposals is not primarily to reduce the tax burden at particular points of the scale so much as to raise the share of the national income taken by tax revenue in a way which is not so damaging as that which appertains at present. For a reduction in the overall tax bill

35

we shall have to wait for a reduction in total government expenditure. But the most important point of all is that if by reforming our tax system and reducing our taxes we can encourage a higher rate of growth, all of our people will benefit, those in the lower income groups most of all.

I have deliberately not dealt with the taxation of companies: not because I agree either with corporation tax system or the system which it has replaced. Indeed on this question my views are precisely the same as those I expressed when I spoke to the British Association twelve years ago. But I have not dealt with this issue today because I believe that what needs to be tackled urgently is the taxation of individuals.

Our problems as a nation all flow fundamentally from the fact that our level of production is neither high enough nor increasing rapidly enough. The measures taken over the last three years which have included massive increases in taxation have resulted in an even slower growth. This has got to be reversed and so too have the policies which have produced this result. The biggest single contribution which can be made to this end is to reduce taxation and particularly the taxation of incomes. If this is done we shall all benefit, both as individuals and as a nation.

3

A T Peacock & J Wiseman

Measuring the efficiency of government expenditure

The title of this paper is misleading, in that we do not have any simple unambiguous measures to offer by which the efficiency of government spending might be assessed. Indeed, we would assert that there are no such measures. Efficiency is a many-sided concept, and statements about it normally incorporate personal judgments of value that are often left implicit. It does not follow that interest in efficiency is pointless, or that policies concerned to promote efficiency of particular kinds cannot be useful. But such specific measures need always to be related to a context that embraces efficiency in all its aspects. Failure to appreciate this is responsible for much of the misunderstanding and disagreement associated with public debate on the topic.

We shall attempt to set out what seems to us to be an appropriate framework for the understanding of the notion of efficiency in relation to government expenditure, and comment upon some of the tests of efficiency now being used in Britain or other countries. This requires consideration of the aspects of efficiency that are normally thought of as the concern of economists, of efficiency as a political concept, and of both these sets of ideas in relation to what might be called *procedural* efficiency—efficiency, that is, in the parliamentary, etc., controls operating at various stages of the expenditure decision-process (budget cycle). We shall find that there are conceptual and practical problems to be solved in respect of all of these, and that their resolution is the more difficult in that problems which can be described and discussed separately cannot in fact be solved separately. Nevertheless, some effort at understanding is called for: an appreciation of the complexities is the necessary first step towards sophistication in control procedures.

There is ample statistical evidence that what would be conventionally regarded as expenditure by public authorities in developed countries has become an increasingly important factor in the structure of the economy. From what is known of future plans or projections of government spending in developed countries over the next decade, it would seem probable that two important trends will continue:

(a) Government expenditure as a proportion of GNP will remain fairly stable in those countries in which it is relatively high, and is likely to increase as a proportion of GNP in those countries in which it is relatively low, thus reducing the present dispersion. The explanation of this phenomenon lies in the probability of growing involvement of government in welfare programmes, e.g. in Canada and in the USA, which have so far been the primary concern of the private sector or of provincial (state) and local governments.

(b) There is also likely to be a move towards more centralization of decision-making in government spending. This is a product of two forces. The first is the desire to develop not only minimum standards of service in particular forms of expenditure but also to some extent to ensure uniformity of provision. The second force is the growing concern with the problem of 'spillover', i.e. the extent to which fiscal operations in one governmental area affect others. One way of coping with this problem is by 'internalizing the externalities', i.e. by creating larger units of government. This 'concentration process', as we have called it elsewhere, may not necessarily be reflected simply in a redefinition of the administrative responsibilities of government, but may also occur through a growing dependence of lower levels of government on financial support received from the centre. (The 'centre' in this case may be the central government, or it may be the 'provincial' or 'state' government providing finance for 'local' or 'parish' government.)

Our problem is not to try to explain the amount, timing or composition of expenditure growth, fascinating though we find the search for uniformities in this area. The actual and expected growth of spending emphasizes the importance of ensuring that what is spent is well spent. Our question is, simply, how can we do it?

I The special problem of government

It is commonly suggested that if government adopted the kind of techniques which result in cost-saving in business, all the advantages of business efficiency could be achieved, and passed on in lower 'prices'—that is, in less taxation for any given level of government 'output'. The idea is not without merit: the recent steps to utilize the experience of firms like Marks and Spencer to improve efficiency in government purchasing, for example, are clearly of potential value. But it is an approach that can have only a limited utility, because the analogy between business and government becomes misleading if pushed very far. An elucidation of the differences is a useful way of explaining the character of the problems with which efficiency in government spending must be concerned.

The analogy derives from the fact that an individual enterprise will normally have a strong incentive to minimize the cost of resources (labour, raw materials and so on) used to produce a given output. Its purpose is to maximize profits, an objective which is within broad limits quantifiable and distinct, and the more successful it is in increasing the margin between the value of output and the cost of inputs, the more 'efficient' the enterprise can be said to be.

There are two general deficiencies in this description. First, it assumes that efficiency from the point of view of the enterprise must imply economic efficiency from the point of view of the community. Second, it ignores the conflicts of interest that may be created by the existence of the corporate enterprise. These are both large subjects in their own right. But their

39

brief elucidation will further our understanding of the related problem of government.

(1) *The competitive market and efficiency in government*

The incentive of a business enterprise to economize, and the contribution of its profit-maximizing activities to the general economic welfare, depend upon the environment within which it operates. The community's interest in the efficiency of enterprises lies in the benefit conferred upon consumers rather than producers. Very generally, this efficiency is going to be best assured if the individual producers are kept conscious of costs by the need to meet competition, and are in no position to 'rig' the market prices of either the goods they sell or the inputs they use. The difficulties met with in the creation and maintenance of such an environment are well enough known. Policies to control monopoly and restrictive practices are an important function of government, and there is no general agreement as to the extent to which the need for size in the interest of technological efficiency conflicts with the need for competition as a guarantee of consumer welfare.

These difficulties become much more prominent in respect of the services provided and inputs purchased by government rather than by enterprises. Commonly, such services and inputs cannot be priced and allocated through competitive markets, and even if they could the nature of the services in question is such as to demand the intervention of government in the pricing process.[1]

To take a topical example, the British Government as an employer of aircraft manufacturers is inevitably in the position of a monopsonist or at least a dominant purchaser: it is unreal to discuss the possible existence of a competitive market in this sector so long as the government retains its present interest. The same is true of many other government purchases. Again,

[1] We shall not concern ourselves here with trading corporations (nationalized industries), which commonly use some form of pricing. It is worth noticing in passing, however, that some of the efficiency problems that we shall discuss (such as how to reproduce the results of competitive conditions) also arise here.

the government frequently purchases goods and services that no one else wants, or at least would be willing to buy in the absence of government involvement. Aircraft research provides an example: the 'value' of such research is to a considerable extent the value placed upon it by government. No one else would be willing to buy it (though private producers may benefit from the resultant 'technological fall-out'). There can be no realistic 'competitive market price' for such purchases of the government.

Similar problems arise in the distribution of government 'output'. For a number of reasons, governments are unwilling to use prices to 'ration' their output of particular services to consumers, much less encourage competition in their provision. Consequently, profitability cannot be used as a guide to efficiency. One reason for this absence of 'rationing by price' lies in the fact that the 'gross' and 'net' benefit from the service may be believed to be different, in that not all the costs and benefits associated with its provision can readily be imputed to individuals. This is not of course a problem unique to the public sector: the classic examples concern the community costs e.g. of water pollution or smoke emission: and these can be generated by either private or governmental activity. Nevertheless, the postulated presence of these 'external' benefits and costs is a common argument for the provision of services by government, and on conditions other than market purchase.

An associated problem arises from the fact that many government services are indivisible. For example, the defence programme is 'consumed' by the whole community. Only one level of provision is possible, and there is no agreed method by which the value of (benefit from) the service can be arrived at and imputed to individual members of the community. It also follows that even those who would not voluntarily contribute towards the provision of such services may not be able to be denied access to them. Market pricing cannot be used to govern efficiency in the provision of such services, to which a 'principle of exclusion' cannot be applied. The level of provision of services, and the allocation of their costs to individual citizens, thus becomes a matter for political bargaining.[1]

We have not yet introduced many relevant complexities. But it must already be apparent that, if we cannot determine either the volume or the value of some kinds of government 'output' (which is implied by the argument so far), then we cannot use conventional 'business enterprise' measures to estimate or control the efficiency of government provision of services without major qualification. Nor are alternatives easy to come by. Those familiar with the National Income Blue Book will know that the contribution of the Government to national output is there recorded along with the output of other goods and services. But they may be surprised to learn that this contribution is assessed as the sum of the wages and salaries of civil servants: that is, output is measured by *cost*. This assumes that an increase in exact proportion in the numbers of civil servants in all grades would increase the measured 'output' of government proportionately if salaries remained unchanged. Again, a cost-reducing innovation (such as computerization) would *reduce* the value of government output. The utility of these measures is not self-evident, nor are they compatible with the concepts of efficiency adopted elsewhere in the economy.

To conclude this section, it is pertinent to point out that the analogy with private enterprise is deficient in another respect. Apart from efficiency in the use of resources for particular purposes, governments are also concerned with those broader (macro-economic) aspects of efficiency that concern the utilization of resources in general—that is, with efficiency in the stimulation of full employment and economic growth. It cannot be assumed that efficiency in the pursuit of these objectives will always contribute to (or be compatible with) efficiency in the provision of particular services, however this is defined.

[1] It is true that indivisibility need not imply that voluntary agreement about the service to be provided cannot be reached, as Buchanan and others have pointed out. But in the case of services such as defence, the administrative costs of trying to arrive at such a solution are likely to be prohibitive.

(2) *Conflict of interest: political 'maximization'*
The second group of difficulties raised by our description of 'business efficiency' concerned the existence of corporate enterprise. This introduces an important possibility of *conflict of objectives*: the separation of ownership and control made possible by limited liability makes inadequate the simple identification of efficiency with calculations of enterprise costs and profits. The interests of management and shareholders can and do diverge: and with that divergence must come a difference in their views of efficient (maximizing) behaviour. As elsewhere, competition provides some sort of a check on undue departures from the pursuit of profit, but efficiency within the corporation is obviously not a simple notion.

Without wishing to press the comparison unduly, it can be observed that the existence of other objectives is even more relevant to efficiency in the provision of services by government. The decisions of government must be political decisions (since governments are political entities). This being so, it is not fruitful to try to distinguish 'economic' and 'political' objectives, as though they could produce independent efficiency criteria. Rather, economic considerations must be related to political objectives and procedures, and efficiency concepts elucidated in relation to both. The point is perhaps most easily illustrated by setting out some possible (likely) other objectives.

In the first place, even if it were possible to exclude those unwilling to pay from the benefit of particular public services, e.g. by charging fees, governments may still choose not to do so, whether because they believe the choice-patterns of individuals to be 'unsatisfactory' or because they regard the provision of particular services at less than cost as a useful means of changing the distribution of income. Such arguments have been relevant to policy decisions in Britain and elsewhere in fields like health and education. More broadly, it may be a cardinal element of policy to sever the nexus between benefits received and the amounts paid by individual citizens for *all* government services, because the distribution of income

43

between citizens generated by market forces is considered un-satisfactory. This is a concept that lies outside the 'business efficiency' approach to spending. It follows from it that those who receive the lowest residuum of net benefits from govern-ment (usually the relatively rich) may have a direct interest in the careful scrutiny of government programmes. The relatively poor, on the other hand, may judge the volume of services provided or of redistribution achieved to be more important measures of government efficiency than the detailed control of particular types of spending.

This leads directly to an even broader objective. Even if conventional measures of 'efficiency' could be used by govern-ments, it does not follow that their policies would become simply 'cost-conscious'. Governments are not in the business of selling products for money. Rather, in the graphic phrase of Professor Downs, they 'sell policies for votes'. So long as they wish to remain in power, their policies must be directed to re-taining or attracting voting support. We have just given ex-amples that make clear that this cannot be simply a matter of cost-consciousness: it is likely to be less so, for example, the wider is the franchise. Nor, happily, does such voting support easily become a matter of simple bribery. Moral considerations apart, the indivisibility of many public services means that most citizens are not easily persuaded that the benefits they receive from government are more valuable than their tax burdens: they do not think of themselves as 'consumers' of defence or public administration. But the central point re-mains: a policy may be 'efficient' in some technical sense, but 'inefficient' (or believed to be so) in a political one, in that its implementation would lose the governing party votes.

Finally, it has to be recognized that the political process is a continuous one, making provision for the reconciliation of the interests and objectives of voters, government, Parliament and bureaucracy. Efficiency concepts need to be concerned with this process. Accordingly, the discussion of actual procedures concerned with efficiency in the following sections will follow the course of the budget cycle, dealing first with efficiency in

44

formulating *plans* for spending, then with the provision of *information* about the plans once formulated, and finally with the *implementation* of approved plans.

II Formulating spending plans

(1) *Overall control*

It is not too difficult to develop a sophisticated theoretical model that could guide the formulation of government spending plans at both an aggregate and a detailed level. One might for example follow the recently developed theory of economic policy *à l'hollandaise*, and specify an 'objective function' which identifies changes in social welfare with the behaviour of important economic magnitudes such as the rate of economic growth. One could then maximize this function, subject to various economic and institutional constraints which the policy-formulator takes as data. In principle at least, the problems of efficiency discussed in previous sections could be dealt with by introducing the various objectives into the model and assigning appropriate weights.

Without doubt, this mode of thinking makes for understanding and consistency in budget-making. But intractable problems arise when we try to translate the objective function into working rules, or to persuade a legislature to accept the outcome of such a procedure for the size and character of the budget without objection. The different political parties, and indeed individual members of Parliament, would support different objective functions and weightings—assuming, that is, that they could ever be persuaded to frame their argument or formulate their views in a way that made discussion of objective functions meaningful. Other things apart, the degree of technical (politico-economic) understanding of those concerned may be inadequate, and even if it is not, they might be expected to retain a healthy scepticism as to the economist's ability to value the parameters in the model of the economy correctly, much less to assign appropriate values to things

45

important to the decision-maker but clearly outside the economist's technical competence. Equally, they must be expected to question the kind of assumptions that normally underlie such models—such as the assumption that the services to be provided will, unless otherwise determined by the objective function, in fact be provided 'efficiently'.

In consequence, practice diverges considerably from this theoretical 'ideal'. The first result is that the control of overall spending becomes separated procedurally from the planning of individual programmes or projects. At the general level, governments have tried to induce legislatures to accept relatively simple 'rules' which can then be treated as in some sense self-evident, or at the minimum can operate as a warning to departments of the possible need to modify their plans.

Historically, the usual method of obtaining acceptance of general 'rules' of this kind has been to appeal to precepts of 'careful household management', or 'sound business practice'. Given for example the notions that there is a limit to the amount of taxation that is politically acceptable, and that borrowing is only 'sound' if it increases the nation's capital stock, it is not too difficult to derive budgetary rules which inhibit too rapid a growth of spending, especially on current account. These concepts of financial 'soundness' have been and still are of importance in developed countries, and particularly in Continental Europe: they encourage governments and administrations to exercise considerable ingenuity in at least appearing to obey the rules. But the rules themselves have become increasingly suspect, both because (as we have seen) the precepts of 'sound finance' are of restricted relevance to the objectives of government, and because of their conflict with evolving technical (economic) concepts about the role of government in the economy.

Thus, while it is still established practice for governments to accept the need to relate spending plans to the idea of a revenue constraint, 'sound financing' is less usually associated with a balanced budget or a 'correct' division between expenditure on

46

current and on capital account. 'Efficiency' in determining the size of the total budget has to be judged by its predicted impact (for growth and economic stability) on the behaviour of the whole economy. Acceptance of this macro-economic view of expenditures has shown itself in a new attitude to expenditure planning which sees as the crucial magnitude the relation between the rate of growth of the economy and the rate of growth of public spending. Evidence of the acceptance of this new concept of 'soundness' is to be found, not only in budget speeches in Britain and elsewhere but also in the first National Plan, which pays particular attention to the need to provide justification for a higher rate of growth of government claims over resources than the predicted growth rate of the economy as a whole.

The 'rule' embodied in the first National Plan is different in *form* from earlier expenditure norms, but hardly more sophisticated in result. It takes the projected growth rate of the economy as a basis, and places a limit on the permitted growth of public spending that is related to (but higher than) this predicted growth rate.

A more sophisticated practical example of the new 'expenditure orthodoxy' is the concept of the 'structural budget margin' which is used in the Netherlands and is associated with the economist and former Minister of Finance, Professor Zijlstra.[1]

The 'margin' is simply the amount of funds available to the government either to increase expenditure rates or to reduce tax rates, or both, and is calculated by assuming that government expenditure is 'permitted' to grow at the same rate as money national income and that taxes are some function of the rate of increase in money national income. In the Dutch case the percentage increase in taxes (t) is assumed to be greater than the percentage increase in money national income because, even with fixed tax rates, the progressivity of the tax

[1] Our account is based on the excellent paper by Professor Theodor Stevers, 'Some Aspects of the Impact of Social Developments on Public Finance', *Le Budget Aujourd'hui* (1967).

schedules will ensure that taxes increase faster than national income. Thus

$$t = (e - 1)y$$

where

t = percentage increase in taxes
y = percentage increase in money national income

and

e = elasticity of taxes with respect to money national income

it being assumed that $e > 1$.

The margin can be calculated as follows:

$$M_1 = yG_0 + tT_0$$

where

M_1 = margin in year 1
G_0 = government expenditure in year 0
T_0 = taxes in year 0;

therefore

$$M_2 = y(1 + y)G_0 + t(1 + y)T_0 = (1 + y)M_1$$

$$\cdot$$
$$\cdot$$
$$\cdot$$

$$M_n = (1 + y)^{n-1}M_1.$$

Thus if

$$y = \cdot 03, \ e = 1\cdot 1 \ (\text{thus } t = \cdot 003), \ G_0 = 100$$
$$T_0 = 105,$$

then

$$M_1 = 4\cdot 02$$
$$M_2 = 4\cdot 33 \ (\text{app.})$$

$$\cdot$$
$$\cdot$$
$$\cdot$$

$$M_n = (1\cdot 03)^{n-1}4\cdot 02.$$

The *structural budget margin* has implications for efficiency in its economic policy sense, and also in its politico-procedural one.

There is a latent conflict between the use of the budget for implementing structural (growth) policy and its contribution to the counter-cyclical (short-term price and employment stability) objective. In broad terms, Netherlands' governments

48

until 1964 took the margin to imply that government expenditure should rise no faster than national income, and they could claim reasonable success in achieving this aim. However, the 'structural' aim sometimes came into conflict with the 'cyclical' one. Because of the progressivity of the Netherlands' tax system, tax yields with unchanged tax rates tend to rise faster than national income. Thus, the government had to face the dilemma of adjusting tax rates downwards, which might weaken the built-in flexibility of the tax structure so important for fiscal policy, or of risking the danger of 'being in funds' and being subjected to increasing pressure to spend. The general philosophy appears to have been to use monetary rather than budgetary policy to maintain stability, on the ground that it can operate more quickly. But the underlying conflict remains, and has destroyed the value of the procedure as an 'automatic' efficiency device from 1965 on. Simply, the value of the system has been undermined since 1964 by a 15% rise in wage costs in one year, followed by an average rise of 10% over the following three years. The effect of this on government spending is direct: government salaries are tied to those in the private sector. No norms of budgetary efficiency can operate independently of this kind of breakdown of other aspects of stabilization policy. This same period also exemplifies the latent conflict of efficiency in its economic and political aspects. When Socialists replaced Liberals in the governing coalition, they accepted the concept of the *margin* in principle, but also pursued policies explicitly designed to increase the share of government in gross national product.

But these difficulties are inherent in any kind of budgetary procedures concerned with efficiency. Despite them, there is good reason to argue that the Netherlands' approach is more conducive to effective overall control than the British one. The latter runs into special difficulty if there is a disparity between the projected and the actual growth rate of the economy—as has in fact happened over the Plan period. In such circumstances, it proves politically as well as technically very difficult, if not impossible, to cut back the 'promised' rate of expenditure growth, and any resultant deflationary adjustment (as in the 1965 balance of payments crisis) has to be made largely by cutting back the claims on resources of the private sector. Thus, while it provides no automatic reconciliation of 'growth' and 'stabilization' efficiency, the use of the structural budget margin, with the 'planning' growth rate firmly geared to past performance, would make for a more realistic control of expenditure than has recent British policy.[1]

There is also need to reconcile the size of the public sector, as determined by the *structural budget margin* calculation, and efficiency at the less general level of individual spending programmes. Conceptually, if the 'guidelines' used to accept or reject individual programmes are themselves 'efficient', then the 'right' total of public expenditures would be given by the sum of expenditures on 'acceptable' projects. In such circumstances, what need is there for other guidelines, concerned with the rate at which the public sector 'should' grow relative to any postulated growth in GNP? This is a question to which we shall return.

When we turn to politico-procedural questions, the major difficulty would seem to be that of persuading executives and legislatures that the *structural budget margin* provides a control technique that is both comprehensible and worthwhile. It has not been unsuccessful in the Netherlands, a country with some reputation for sophistication in such matters. Whether it could be made successful in Britain, at least in present conditions, is perhaps more open to doubt. It would require an unusual degree of control and responsibility from ministers: but they are beginning to be faced by the need for some such discipline in any event. Perhaps more important, the use of the *structural budget margin* might do something to restore the paramount authority of the Chancellor of the Exchequer on expenditure matters. This might be good from the point of view of efficiency

[1] On the whole question of history of fiscal policy within the general context of economic policy in the Netherlands during this period, see F. Hartog, 'Economic Policy in the Netherlands, 1949–61' in Kirschen (ed.), *Economic Policy in our Time* (Amsterdam, 1964), and also Stevers, *op. cit.*

in overall control of the budget. Whether it would be acceptable to other ministers with their own fish to fry is perhaps a more debatable topic.

(2) *Individual spending plans*

It would be easy to imagine, judging from the documents produced by individual ministries, that expenditure planning for individual services is a simple costing process, once standards of service have been laid down. Thus projections of expenditure on health services embody estimates of the utilization of the NHS *inter alia* by age group; they must therefore be based essentially upon population projections. But even if standards of service are roughly agreed (assuming they can be defined in the first place!), it is clear that a rational procedure must take account of several other factors. First of all, assuming that factor prices remain constant, it is a moot point how far the cost per unit of service will vary with utilization. This can only be decided upon by detailed investigation. Secondly, there is no reason to suppose the *relative* factor prices will remain fixed. Thus if in the long run there are alternative employment opportunities for potential and existing doctors which are more attractive than working for the NHS, even the strong bargaining position of the government in the market for professional services will not necessarily prevent a relative rise in salary scales. It follows that statements that we 'face a shortage of doctors and nurses' is only another way of saying that the government is unwilling or unable either to offer the market price, and thus to increase the cost of the service in order to preserve existing standards, or alternatively to alter the factor-mix (technique of provision of NHS services) in such a way that it can preserve standards without a rise in relative factor prices.

The general point being made is that, *within a budget constraint*, there is no getting round the problem of measuring the opportunity-cost of individual government services. The cost of maintaining or improving standards in, say, health or education, must be measured in terms of the alternatives foregone (loss of resources to other community uses) and no amount of sophistication in estimating procedure will make projections using internal (technical) criteria related only to the service itself capable of dispensing with the pains of choice. The point is a simple one, but important enough to bear reiteration. Technical projections of the 'needs' of particular services may be of value in illuminating some of the future implications of policies already extant, but their utility for policy *decisions* is restricted by the fact that they permit of no (or inadequate) adaptation of the service itself to evolving conditions and scarcities. Thus, 'shortages' of manpower or other resources, calculated by reference to the technical requirements of individual services, must be expected to sum to totals that it is beyond the means of the economy to provide.

The most widely publicized method of appraisal developed in recent years to take care of these problems, and to bring the general scarcity of resources and the need for choice into the decision-process, is known as cost-benefit analysis. This type of analysis has now been applied to everything from the Dutch system of dykes to syphilis control programmes in the USA. What it does can best be explained by analogy with capital budgeting in business. An enterprise interested in a new capital project will want to know whether it will 'pay'. The cost of the investment and the net returns from it will be compared with the alternative use of the funds to finance it. In highly sophisticated analysis of the Discounted Cash Flow kind, returns which accrue in the future will be discounted to the present after allowing for future tax obligations, and alternative uses of funds will be carefully scrutinized. Cost-benefit analysis in government adopts essentially the same procedure but the analogy with business, as should already be clear, cannot be pushed too far.

An example may help here. Imagine that the government is contemplating building a barrage carrying a road across an estuary, and that there are two possible locations for it. The capital cost of each alternative plus any accompanying road improvements is the same. Possible benefits are the shortening of road distances and the by-passing of towns, so that both direct costs of travel and congestion costs are reduced to motorists and operators of commercial vehicles. Again, let it be assumed that the time-stream of these benefits and their amount is the same in both cases. However, one difference is assumed: the first barrage will produce a diversion in the estuary flow which would reduce the size of a wildfowl preserve, while the second, while not reducing the size of the preserve would destroy a public bathing beach.

Clearly, the appraisal is a much more complicated exercise than for business. In estimating benefits we have to add to the difficulties of forecasting and computing the value of the reduction in travel and in congestion costs through traffic flow analysis, the problem of incorporating the intangible 'dis-benefits': the reduction in the size of the bird sanctuary in one case and the destruction of a beach in the other. It is clearly possible conceptually to place a money value on the fall in costs to the community of the change in the road conditions, though the valuation of savings in journey-time and of the 'benefits' of traffic generated by the crossing create practical problems of considerable difficulty. But it is a question of one's point of view when it comes to relative valuation of amenity. If one is an ornithologist who dislikes bathing, one's valuation of the alternatives is different from that of a bather who has no love for ducks. What is important is the realization that *any* valuation of amenity must rest upon arbitrary assumptions about the weight to be attached to *individuals'* preferences. We must not be bamboozled into believing that there is a technical answer which can be worked out by an official in the Ministry of Land and Natural Resources or by Town and Country Planners, even if we are prepared in the last analysis to leave valuation to government servants in the hope that they will pay attention to different points of view.

But let us assume for a moment that these valuation problems have been solved, and that we have got agreed figures for the time-stream of benefits and costs associated with each project. We now need to turn the two sets of figures into comparable form, which means in the first instance to find present values for the streams in question. There would be wide agreement that benefits accruing only in the future are less valuable than benefits accruing now. But at what rate of interest should we discount? A business anxious for quick returns may adopt a high rate of discount, but it is commonly argued that as a government is concerned with returns to the community at large, it has to take into account, for example, the welfare of any project to future generations. This has been interpreted to mean that the government would normally discount the future at a much lower rate than private enterprise. Again, it must be noted that the choice of a discount rate will depend upon a choice as to *whose preferences are to be given the most weight.* Just as there can be different individual evaluations of amenity, so there can be different assessments of the relative value of present and future consumption. The introduction of a 'social rate of time discount' into technical (economic) discussion is analytically convenient, but we should not ignore the fact that it is a means of sweeping an intractable and important problem under the carpet. Adopting the preference of the policy-maker in this regard is to defer to what one hopes will be an informed judgment: but it does not follow that those preferences have some 'scientific' justification.

So far, we have taken no direct account of the fact that the implementation of either of the barrage projects of our illustration would use resources that are in consequence lost to the private sector of the economy. This would not be a difficulty if we could agree upon the social discount rate, since we would then implement all those projects which were expected to produce a present value of benefits in excess of costs, and both the total size and the structure of public expenditures would be determined. But we have just agreed that such an agreement is not to be expected, depending as it does upon agreement between individuals as to their value judgments about the 'good society'. An alternative is not easily found. Following the analogy with private investment, the most frequent suggestion is that the public project should be undertaken if its rate of return is at least as high as that of an alternative private investment, and that the 'appropriate' measure of this rate of return is the borrowing rate of government. But this is dubious, for several reasons. Apart from the obvious difficulty that the government can and does influence the rate in question, it is not clear why this particular means of raising funds should be chosen as appropriate. There are a whole series of other policies that the government could adopt: instead of raising funds on the capital market, it might raise taxes, cut other programmes, or simply expand credit. Since raising a loan at the current borrowing rate is only one of the many ways of financing a barrage investment, a decision as to whether the investment is 'worth while' cannot be made simply by reference to the ruling borrowing rate, which is only one possible way of computing the 'cost'. (For example, if we imagine that the barrage is financed by a tax which cuts private consumption by exactly the amount of its yield, should we assume that the barrage need not yield *any* return because no *income-yielding* assets are being displaced?)

In the light of all these difficulties, Prest and Turvey have concluded that the task of devising policy-relevant cost-benefit studies is like trying to unscramble an omelette.[1] We would not disagree with this conclusion. But we would also agree that it does not follow that such studies, used intelligently and with discretion, have no role to play as an efficiency device in expenditure planning. Their contribution, and dangers, might be summarized as follows:

Their great positive contribution, at least potentially, lies in the fact that cost-benefit studies do direct attention to all the problems relevant to expenditure decisions about public projects. In principle, therefore, the approach must be more interesting and valuable than simple 'technical' projections of the kind described earlier. Indeed, it has been argued by one authority that as manpower forecasting techniques become

[1] Prest and Turvey, 'Cost-Benefit Analysis', in *Surveys of Economic Theory*, vol. III (Royal Economic Society, 1965).

more sophisticated, the different techniques become reconcilable and from a policy point of view complementary.[1]

At the same time, the value of the cost-benefit technique, now and in the future, will depend upon the sophistication with which it is used and upon adequate recognition of its dangers. We have drawn attention to the considerable problems of valuation concerned with intangibles, with time preference, and with the opportunity cost of lost private investment. To these we would add at least one other major category, already referred to in Section I(1). This concerns the assessment of the benefits and costs that a project generates for 'society', but which cannot be imputed to (directly valued by) individuals.

If all these evaluations are made simply by policy-makers, the technique will be in danger of becoming no more than a rationalization of their own judgments of value. This is the more important when we look at the technique also from the viewpoint of efficiency in its *political* aspect. The imputation of values is unlikely to remain independent of the (political) process of arriving at them. At the extreme, if a minister is left to value the categories in question, the cost-benefit technique may become no more than a formalization of his or her existing prejudices. There is little point in deciding, say, to electrify the railway line from London to Glasgow, and then using a suitably valued cost-benefit study to 'prove' the decision 'right'. The danger is the greater in that, as we have seen, the technique is not formally consistent with the *structural budget margin* approach to overall efficiency: there must be room for ministerial manœuvre pending the evolution of agreed techniques of evaluation so that some kind of 'cut-off-rate' could sensibly be applied to the totality of possible projects.

A major difficulty in the way of this necessary generalization is the fact that the 'intangibles' thrown up by different types of public sector activity are very different in nature. To cite but one example, how are we to bring together the evaluation of amenities of the kind earlier described, the 'social benefit' from

[1] M. Blaug, 'Approaches to Educational Planning', *Economic Journal*, June 1967.

the provision of a particular kind of education, and the 'benefit' of a pound earned abroad rather than at home through a programme designed to improve the balance of payments?

Taken as a group, these arguments suggest that the major value of cost-benefit studies, at least in the foreseeable future, will lie not in providing agreed 'solutions' to decisions about project planning, but rather in providing a more informed body of knowledge about the detailed implications of particular decisions, and through time at least some kind of check on the consistency of decisions as between broadly similar projects. This being so, it is important that the projects be designed and presented to provide not simply numbers, but also a 'shopping list' description of the relevant benefits and costs and of the way in which the evaluation has been attempted. This is also useful for the proper use of the technique in relation to *ex post* evaluation: a matter to which we shall return.

III Presentation of information on spending

We have been concerned so far with efficiency in the drawing up of expenditure plans. This could be treated as essentially an economic matter, though one in which we would argue that political considerations do enter into so-called 'valuation' and other problems. The next stage of the budget cycle is essentially political: it is concerned with the parliamentary approval of expenditure plans. The questions of concern are: What opportunity should be given for Parliament to discuss the proposals placed before it? and, related to this: In what form should expenditure proposals be presented?

The first question is a very large one and can only be touched on here. As is well known, our parliamentary procedure in budgeting is very different from that in other countries. Majority rule coupled with a government directly answerable to Parliament offers no incentive either to public officials or to members of the Cabinet to seek elaborate scrutiny of expenditure plans. The way to political advancement for the individual MP does not lie in his performance in the Select Committee on Estimates or the Committee of Public Accounts or the Committee on Nationalized Industries. In this, he is in a position very different from, e.g., that of his American counterpart. Nor is any additional compensation by way of prestige or payment offered for such service. Small wonder then that the pressure for improvement in research and other services which would enable individual MP's to probe expenditure proposals is mild and sporadic, and usually emanates from those in opposition. Nothing short of a constitutional change will produce a situation in which Parliament, as distinct from the government, will have the right to demand justification of, say, the use of a discount rate of 8% by the Treasury in the appraisal of investment projects.

The form of presentation of expenditure data is thus a function of political necessity. This shows itself in the fact that data must be presented in a fashion complying with the relevant legislation. In the case of Britain, the Financial Statement meets this requirement. But, it might reasonably be asked, why not bring technical (economic) efficiency and political responsibility together by presenting the information in a fashion that is also related to the relevant technical objectives? This apparently simple injunction is not easy to carry out in practice, for reasons that we can do no more than outline here. Apart from the fact that (as we have pointed out at length) neither objectives nor even technical relationships are agreed by all concerned, there is the considerable difficulty that Parliament is a body concerned with the *approval* of expenditure plans, and hence needs information in a form suitable for such approval. This form may and indeed is likely to be very different from the form needed to provide information about (say) the possible contribution of the plans for public expenditures to the stability and growth of the economy over the next five years.

But once having accepted the need to provide a public explanation, e.g. of the use of the budget for the achievement of stability and growth, it follows that some attempt to relate expenditure plans to these objectives must be made. In Britain, this has been recognized in the recent Treasury reforms in the

58

presentation of both the Financial Statement and the Supply Estimates in an alternative classification following national income conventions. (This is again evidence of the presence, at least in spirit, of the 'new orthodoxy' discussed earlier in British fiscal politics.)

There are three respects, however, in which British practice differs from, if it does not lag behind, the practice in other developed countries. The first is in the quantity of supporting documents of a semi-popular character which surround the discussion of the budget and its place in economic planning. It is little short of a scandal that there is no convenient document in Britain similar to the Netherlands Budgetary Memorandum, the US and French Budget in Brief, or their Swedish counterpart, which contain in one handy form the budget speech, the trends in budget receipts and expenditures over some years, and some explanation of the reflection of official policies in the structure and amount of spending. This is the least the taxpayer has a right to expect.

The second is more controversial. Several other countries publish the official short-term forecasts and/or projections of the economy in which the place of government expenditure is clearly shown. If the 'structural budget margin' approach is a useful way of focusing discussion on essential issues of policy, then it must follow that it is possible to relate expenditure plans to total spending. It seems more than likely that we, too, shall have to resume the practice of revealing the government's hand, despite the influential Treasury argument that a country heavily dependent on economic relations with foreigners can ill afford to allow its officials to be too explicit about their view of future economic events. But it will be appreciated that 'efficiency' in this context concerns a delicate balance of judgment about both technical and political relationships and desiderata.

The third raises even more difficult issues of a constitutional character. In common with other countries, legislative approval must be given in Britain to expenditure and tax proposals, but in Britain this does not extend to the precise form in which these are presented. Elsewhere, for example in Germany and Italy, the form of the budget is a matter for definition in a written constitution. In the former country, considerable problems of drafting have arisen in attempting to define the nature of budgetary policy designed to promote economic stability in constitutional provisions. Whereas it is true that it is asking for trouble to attempt to define, say, full employment in a constitutional or legislative document,[1] as the Germans are finding, we might very well consider in this country whether the time has not come to define more precisely the responsibilities of the executive in providing information on budgetary matters and on expenditure proposals in particular to Parliament and to the public at large.

IV The execution of expenditure plans

Plans are formulated, approved, and once blessed or at least condoned by Parliament, they have to be carried out. The fundamental question is, how can we be sure that they are carried out efficiently?

In the traditional sense, efficiency has been equated with the fulfilment of the intentions of Parliament. The mechanism designed to achieve this has been the firm establishment of an efficient accounting and audit system. We take this for granted in Britain, and with it the *regular* presentation of audited Finance Accounts. In consequence there is less emphasis than in the foreign literature on public finance upon 'rules' of budgeting designed to achieve the same end. In this country, the system of *ex post* financial control is coupled with the opportunity given to the legislature through the Public Accounts Committee, advised by the Comptroller and Auditor General, to investigate 'extravagance and waste'. The common complaint made about this system is that the observations and

---

[1] It is understood that the famous clause in the National Insurance Act, 1946, which allows the Treasury to vary the insurance contributions in order to maintain 'a high and stable level of employment' took some weeks to agree and to draft.

criticisms of the Committee come too late in the day to do anything constructive. On the other hand, as has been persuasively argued by Mr Normanton in his erudite and fascinating study of the subject: 'auditors are not stuffed watchdogs; they must inspire respect not by their presence alone but by the evidence of their alertness'.[1] In short, audit can be a form of preventive control provided that there is continuity in the system of public accountability.

Nevertheless, an economist cannot be content with this way of looking at efficiency, however important it is to ensure that money is spent in authorized ways. It is certainly the case that auditing practices may produce side-benefits in the form of improved cost control and management techniques. On the other hand, as stressed in our earlier discussion, efficiency has a particular meaning to the economist concerned essentially with efficiency in resource-use. There is little reason to expect efficiency in terms of accountability to be identical with efficiency in its resource-use sense.

As previously argued, finding out the relative efficiency of a government service assumes that it is possible to select measures of output and input in circumstances in which output is not sold. Faced with this situation, it is common practice to concentrate on cost analysis. For example, let us assume that an investigation shows that in a given local authority area the larger the size of a secondary school, as measured by numbers of pupils, the lower the cost per pupil. Ignoring the difficulties encountered in defining and measuring cost, the policy conclusion which may be drawn is that waste of resources could be reduced by replacing smaller schools over time by larger ones. But this argument implicitly assumes that the unit of 'output' is the pupil. This is clearly a matter for debate. The supporters of smaller schools might argue that the higher costs per pupil result in a 'better' education as judged, say, by examination results and the 'more intimate' atmosphere. The first argument could presumably be tested by some

[1] E. L. Normanton, *The Accountability and Audit of Governments* (Manchester Univ. Press, 1966), p. 83.

acceptable measure of performance; it is empirically verifiable. A test of intimacy is another matter! Both arguments obviously rest on value judgments about the aims of education. The supporters of larger schools are not obliged to accept them and might offer the rejoinder that ability to pass examinations is a product of inheritance as well as environment. (In economist's jargon, the inputs provided by nature have not been costed!)

Therefore, what appears to be a technical exercise in accounting turns out to be meaningless because the objectives of policy have not been specified, far less agreed. Governments frequently take refuge in vague statements of objectives such as 'sound' education policy or 'satisfactory standard of health provision', while what is needed is their translation into proximate criteria which offer the prospect of measurement. Even if measurement is difficult, if not well nigh impossible, it is better to be clear about what one is doing than to be landed with a precise but totally wrong answer produced by some accounting sleight-of-hand.

It will be appreciated that these comments come close to a repetition of those made in II(2) concerning the use of technical criteria in expenditure planning. This is not of course surprising: one would expect similar techniques and problems to arise in planning the attainment of particular objectives and in verifying success. Thus, parallel with the development of cost-benefit analysis as a planning technique, there have been similar developments in execution and verification methods.

From what can be culled from official documents relating to the UK, it would appear that we are only just beginning to consider the introduction of 'programme' or 'performance' budgeting as means of improving our knowledge of the productivity (efficiency) of government services. This relatively new technique attempts an approximation to productivity measurement in the private sector by specifying and, where possible, quantifying the objectives of any particular government programme, and then examining the costs of achieving them. A very interesting attempt has been made to measure the productivity of British higher education by this method by Miss Woodhall and Dr Blaug. They adopt four different indexes of output: the number of graduates (the 'naïve' index), the number of graduates weighted by length of course (the 'educational' index), the number of graduates with a weight to Arts graduates (the 'cultural' index) and the number of graduates weighted according to potential earnings (the 'economic' index). They then compare the movement of these indexes with the movement in costs through time and, fortunately, given their definitions of output, reach an unequivocal result because between 1938 and 1962, the index of cost rises at a faster rate than any of the indexes of output. Naturally, academics disturbed by the conclusion that productivity in higher education has fallen, have fastened on to one of the major difficulties in all productivity studies: how to adjust for quality changes. In the example given it could be argued that a degree in 1962 is of 'higher value' than one in 1938 due to advances in knowledge and improvements in teaching methods. Even so, this approach is obviously much more satisfactory than mere costing exercises.

Clearly, the economists' attempts to identify production functions within the public sector offer a useful way of appraising programmes already in operation, but as in the case of auditing procedures, the justification for *ex post* analysis lies in the 'pay off' achieved in the design of new programmes. Indeed, while programme budgeting implies that simple costing procedures are inadequate as a check on performance, it should itself perhaps be treated logically as a part of the process of formulation as well as the execution of expenditure plans. However it is treated, it gives rise to some important difficulties as well as to policy problems which deserve at least brief mention.

In the first place, the attempt to relate inputs to outputs runs up against major statistical difficulties because the necessary classification of data cuts right across traditional administrative classifications. A very good example of this is provided by Mr Williams, in his CAS paper, in attempting to isolate the particular functions of the Home Office and then to associate with each of them the relevant inputs.[1] A further conceptual problem arises when it is discovered that some inputs cannot be allocated to particular outputs or functions because they have a 'common service' element. But these statistical and conceptual difficulties suggest in themselves that the administrative structure itself may need reform if it does not follow functional lines. But it is easy to imagine the 'built-in' resistance within the administration if a more logical framework were contemplated. Nor is such resistance entirely misplaced: it hardly needs argument that efficiency in its political and procedural aspects may here run counter to efficiency in the technical sense now being discussed. The political role of departments, for example, clearly cannot be subsumed within the functional relationships necessary for performance budgets.

The point is important enough to require developing, as a culminating illustration of the complexity of the concept of efficiency in the context of public spending. It is clear that a tightening of control and co-ordination must facilitate the technically efficient use of programme budgeting, and that the use of the technique is therefore facilitated by centralization in decision-making. Cost-benefit analysis (a logical extension of performance budgeting) has the same characteristic. A decision about the evaluation of the barrage schemes in our earlier illustration, for example, will be easier if it can be taken directly by a central authority with a single 'objective function', than if all the interested sub-authorities' needs must be consulted (it is easy to think of twenty bodies who would be interested in such a scheme in Britain), to say nothing of the need to ascertain the views of the local populace. But of course it is precisely in these circumstances that the 'business efficiency' analogy is most dangerous. Decentralization of decision-taking may be regarded as an end in itself: a necessary 'input' for

[1] Alan Williams, *Output Budgeting and the Contribution of Micro-Economics to Efficiency in Government* (HMSO, 1967; Centre for Administrative Studies, 1967).

efficient political decision-making. Equally, such decentralization may promote efficiency in other ways: it could be argued that in the defined circumstances it may be the closest available substitute for the discipline of the market-place and the process of competition in the provision of public goods. Those who threaten to 'vote with their feet' may help to keep local governments 'on their toes'.

Once again, then, we end in compromise. Performance budgeting is a useful technique, whose use in Britain could certainly be extended with value. But its contribution to efficiency in public spending must be a restricted one, and must be understood in relation to the broader environment.

V Some conclusions

The reader might be forgiven for deciding that the purpose of the paper has been to start from the simple idea of government expenditure efficiency and to take pleasure in complicating it. But we would hope that the argument has demonstrated convincingly that too *simpliste* a view of efficiency in government spending is likely to do as much harm as good.

Efficiency in the context of public expenditures must have a different connotation from efficiency in business: it is concerned with a *political* decision process, and has political, economic and procedural implications which are logically distinguishable but not always separable in practice. To cite only one example, we have argued that the utility of cost-benefit studies or performance budgeting, and also the very valuations imputed to particular benefits or costs in such studies, are not independent of the political and administrative environment through which decisions are taken.

This is not to say that efficiency control is impossible or should not be attempted: far from it. There are indeed a number of ways in which we have suggested that British procedures for the control of public spending might be improved. At the level of overall planning control, some move to relate total spending explicitly to *growth experience*, and perhaps following the Dutch concept of the *structural budget margin*, would be an improvement upon the present situation, which forces adjustment for stabilization purposes upon the private sector and has recently facilitated the presentation of reduced *rates of growth* of public spending as 'cutbacks'. At the more detailed level of expenditure planning, there is scope for the development of cost-benefit analysis, subject to appropriate safeguards. Specifically there is need to widen the range of data permitting of sensible *comparative* assessment of public projects, while avoiding the very real danger that the technique may become a simple means of bolstering the existing prejudices of ministers.

When we turn to the presentation of information about spending, the welcome development of the Financial Statement and the Supply Estimates to include alternative classifications should be continued and perhaps extended. But there is also a crying need to follow the example of other developed countries in providing basic budgetary information in a summary and easily comprehended form. There may also be need to accept that there is a balance of advantage in making public the official view (forecast) of the place of the government sector in the development of the economy.

Finally, there is scope for the extension and development of *performance budgeting* of a sophisticated kind (moving towards a cost-benefit 'check' on cost-benefit forecasts?).

But we must not expect too much. Even if all the changes we believe to be improvements were made, the checks on efficiency would still be partial, incomplete, and potentially misleading unless interpreted with sophistication. This is no one's fault, but is in the nature of the problem. The use of a *structural budget margin* must be expected to produce a global expenditure figure which cannot be reconciled technically with detailed expenditure planning through cost-benefit studies, at least in the present or any foreseeable state of knowledge or of political agreement. Parliament cannot expect information to be presented in a form that satisfies legislative, procedural and political control requirements, and yet also fits the categories

66

of an economic model suitable, e.g., for growth planning. And departments and procedures cannot be reorganized structurally around the demands of performance budgeting without doing violence to political objectives such as decentralization and departmental responsibility. Thus, efficiency procedures need constantly to be related to a general environment, to ensure that what seems technically efficient in the specific context is also sensible in the broader one. Also, given the inevitable imperfections of information and inference, it is important that as much information be made available as possible, so that the logic of decisions can be generally appreciated. This applies not only to the improvement of formal budgetary information, but also to, e.g., the manner in which cost-benefit studies are presented: they should give not simply estimates but a detailed explanation of the considerations treated as relevant and the valuation procedures used.

None of this will give us perfect checks on efficiency in public spending. But it might help to direct attention towards the important issues.

4
Sir Harry Page

Local authority capital finance—practices and problems

Local authority capital finance represents an important sector of the national economy; yet, from a purely theoretical or academic point of view, the system is based upon a number of somewhat rough and ready, one might almost say dubious, principles. Despite this, from the point of view of the practitioner—the man involved in the day-to-day job of raising capital funds and meeting capital expenditure—the system in fact works admirably and is considered to be fundamentally sound and well fitted to its purpose, though treasurers may chafe at the externally imposed restraints under which they have to operate. Taking into account the frame of reference against which it must be considered, the system can be said to work well, which is not to say that criticism is resented. There is room for improvement.

But two points need to be stressed: (a) we in local government want a system which recognizes that capital expenditure and finance is a means to an end: the end is good public services, locally and democratically controlled, and we are prepared to pay a price in interest rates, and up to a point, in basic efficiency, rather than see any further attrition of local self-government; and (b) the purpose of this paper is to make clear that when the theoretical concepts which should underlie the system have been defined, and when the broad decisions of policy, based upon the national needs, have been taken, there is still a difficult, though stimulating, practical job to be done in the management of the local authority capital budgets.

Local authority loan debt

What amount of money are we talking about? Appendix 1 gives statistics relating to local authority loan debt which show that the debt in England and Wales has increased from £6,000m to £8,400m between 1961 and 1965—quite a formidable increase. The net debt per head of population has risen from £130 to £176 over the same period.

What reliable criteria are there which will tell us whether or not this is a lot of money? If we look more closely at the loan debt figures we see that the debt of the housing and trading undertakings together is £6,000m of the £8,400m. This portion of the debt is revenue-earning and largely self-supporting even though our housing activities may at the moment be subsidized. There is no doubt that this portion of our debt is not 'burdensome' and is more than covered by the value of real assets if we could ever consider that we might be faced with a 'break-up'.

In terms of debt per head of population £127 of the £176 is for these revenue-earning services. This is not to say that the remainder is unproductive because income is derived from a small proportion of other services.

The absolute amount of debt is perhaps less worrying than the rate of growth and the consequential increase in the annual charge for service of the debt. In 1965, the expenditure of local authorities in England and Wales on interest and repayment amounted to no less than £563m. What is perhaps also a cause for concern—and this point is taken up again later in this paper —is that as a consequence of heavy capital expenditure year after year out of loans, a point is ultimately reached when the annual charge for interest and repayment exceeds the amount of capital expenditure and a policy of financing all such expenditure from revenue would, in fact, have resulted in a lower annual charge. The advantage of spreading expenditure over a period of years has been lost.

Relationship of local authority capital formation to GNP

I am somewhat reluctant to enter too readily into an examination of the relationship of local capital formation with the Gross National Product (GNP) partly because my experience is that the analysis of figures used by the Central Statistical Office is not always by any means on the same lines as the local authorities like to analyse them. Then again, while we have to calculate a GNP it seems to me a rather odd sort of figure, liable to considerable variation according to the definitions we use.

The following table shows local authority capital formation as part of GNP and for good measure compares local government capital expenditure with that of the public corporations.

	Gross National Product	Total gross domestic fixed capital formation			
		Local authorities		Public corporations	
	£ million	£ million	% of GNP	£ million	% of GNP
1955	16,945	538	3·2	654	3·7
1956	18,421	566	3·1	687	3·7
1957	19,516	570	2·9	757	3·9
1958	20,375	535	2·6	785	3·8
1959	21,376	567	2·7	847	4·0
1960	22,768	609	2·7	890	3·9
1961	24,335	684	2·8	932	3·8
1962	25,409	801	3·2	924	3·6
1963	27,003	889	3·3	1,036	3·8
1964	28,910	1,107	3·8	1,197	4·1

(Source—Central Statistical Office)

In 1955 capital expenditure of local authorities was some £540m and accounted for 3·2% of the gross national product. Capital expenditure of the nationalized industries was some £650m, equivalent to 3·7% of GNP. Over the next five years, capital expenditure of the nationalized industries rose steadily by some 30% and absorbed 4% of the GNP in 1959, whereas capital expenditure of local authorities remained fairly constant and the proportion of the GNP had fallen to 2·7% in 1959. In the next quinquennium capital expenditure of the nationalized industries showed a similar increase of some 30%, but the capital expenditure of local authorities increased by over 80% to some £1,100m and by 1964 was absorbing 3·8% of the gross national product. Whereas in 1955 capital expenditure of local authorities was equivalent to 82% of the capital expenditure of the nationalized industries, by 1964 the proportion had risen to over 92%.

Is capital formation at this rate reasonable or not? If it is too high, then the public boards are as subject to criticism as local government.

What is capital expenditure?

I began by admitting that some of our principles and practices have a look of uncertainty about them.

As my first illustration of this let me admit that we are not able to define exactly what we mean by capital expenditure. A recent definition suggests that capital expenditure is that from which the duration of the benefits gained extends beyond the dimension of the accounting period in which the outlay is incurred. One sees what lies behind this definition but in practice it hardly helps because so many reservations have to be made to it. The Institute of Municipal Treasurers and Accountants in devising their Standard Abstract of Accounts have laboured long to define capital expenditure. Bearing in mind that local authorities cannot borrow money without the specific consent, project by project, of a government department, their present definition is: 'All expenditure on an object for which the local authority concerned could reasonably expect to obtain a loan sanction regardless of the way in which it is actually financed', and there are then minor qualifications added to this definition. This seems to me very much to beg the question.

When we build a school or a clinic or a house we are creating a capital asset and incurring capital expenditure, irrespective of the means whereby it is financed. But are we quite so sure that when we build a road or lay a sewer we are creating a capital asset? For local government purposes, I think we are. Any subsequent expenditure, the purpose of which is to maintain the asset in being—painting the buildings or repairing the road—is equally clearly revenue expenditure; but alas for our definition, there is a wide range of expenditure on adaptations and improvements all of which contain an element of maintenance, and indeed there is a good deal of maintenance which from time to time includes an element of improvement, where it is frankly impossible to determine exactly whether or not it is capital expenditure.

The question is whether a definition of capital expenditure has any real significance in local government capital finance.

There are treasurers, of whom I am one, who have never felt that the need to define capital expenditure was important. We may truly say that while we cannot define capital expenditure we clearly recognize it when we see it. If we choose to borrow for an item of expenditure and a government department will give us sanction to do so, may we not leave it at that? In S.E. Lancashire, a good deal of money has been spent on covering old roads, built of granite setts, with hot asphalt carpets—and very successful this policy has been. Manchester chose to meet this expenditure from revenue while other authorities nearby chose to borrow for it. I do not think this matters at all.

Our finances are in no way comparable with those of a public company. There is no real sense in which we can show on one side of our balance sheet our 'capital' and on the other the value, break-up or otherwise, of our assets.

Even the IMTA definition, about which I have expressed reservations, differentiates at a later stage between 'capital outlay'—which covers the real assets (land, buildings and plant), and 'other long-term outlay'—which covers the partly intangible, unsaleable, non-revenue earning assets common to local authorities but less common in other concerns—roads, sewers, sea-defence works and so on. In addition, true deferred charges such as the expenses of local Acts, capitalization of interest, the value of discount on stock issues and so on, are not defined as capital expenditure, but they are nevertheless 'capitalized' by local authorities as a consequence of the method of financing.

Frankly, I question whether local authority capital balance sheets are worth the paper they are printed on. I suspect that they are merely a sop to those who show grave but uninformed concern if there is not a balance sheet which an auditor can certify.

Though we do not have a fixed capital like a commercial concern, we do have a continuous and considerable loan debt which certainly constitutes a capital liability. On the other side of the account we have a vast quantity and range of assets, but what these are 'worth' in relation to our liabilities is quite impossible to ascertain. We could have regular revaluations of these assets and indeed, many, many years ago this was a general local authority practice, but the amount of work involved was so great and the basis of valuation of so many of our assets so hypothetical that the fatuity of this exercise has long since been recognized and the practice abandoned.

Nevertheless, fatuous though it may have been to attempt anything like a positive valuation of our assets, we do still include a figure of what purports to be their value on the credit side of our balance sheet, but we use a most conventional and meaningless method of ascertaining this figure. Our standard practice is to include land, buildings and plant on the basis of historical cost, until the asset goes entirely out of use; the 'unsaleable' items of outlay, our roads, our sewers and the like, we include merely on the basis of historical cost written down over the relevant loan period.

While an accountant may feel that at least this is an attempt at a comparison of assets and liabilities, in practice we must recognize that the exercise is without meaning. An enormous amount of time is spent in a futile attempt to show that our assets are 'worth' more than our liabilities.

We could perhaps treat with some meaning our revenue

earning assets such as our municipal houses and our trading undertakings, but these form only a part of the picture and even if realistic valuations were practicable, to what effect?

Little purpose is served by the creation of balance sheets on the grounds that at some time or another we have to prove that we are a financially sound going concern.

As a result of our determination to stick to the production of a figure for the value of our capital assets we find ourselves forced to capitalize many items of expenditure which are financed from other than borrowed money, in order to build up a fictitious 'value' of assets, and against this we compare only the amount of our outstanding debt.

A definition of capital expenditure is only important to me to separate annual running costs from general non-recurring costs for budget control purposes, and this is a practical issue which causes little trouble.

The control of expenditure from borrowed money

Because I dissociate myself from the fuss about balance sheets, you must not take this to mean that borrowing to finance such capital expenditure as we wish to meet from loans is not closely controlled. On the contrary, local authorities borrowing is closely—some think far too closely—controlled and very carefully administered on a sound practical basis.

To start with, while we can spend what we like from revenue, we cannot borrow money to purchase an asset without the sanction of a government department, usually the Ministry of Housing and Local Government. Exceptionally, we may derive this sanction directly from Parliament in a local Act. In the giving of this sanction, the sanctioning department or the Act of Parliament will specify a period over which the loan we have incurred must be repaid; for example, 30 years for roads, 40 years for most buildings, though oddly enough, 60 years for housing. The establishment of this loan sanction period means that we have to set aside sums from revenue account each year which, by the end of the loan sanction

74

period, will provide a sum for the repayment of the debt. Thus we do not have a permanent capital debt, nor do we therefore need to provide depreciation of our assets in order to set aside funds from revenue for the replacement of the assets when they are obsolete or worn out. There is a real sense in which our annual provision for debt redemption is equivalent to commercial depreciation provision but the distinction is that we are providing for the writing-off of the initial debt and not for the provision of the necessary sums to replace the asset, though there are those among us who argue that we should do so.

Although we must, by law, set aside sums each year to repay the debt over the sanctioned period, we have some discretion about the method by which we calculate the annual sums.

There are those who believe that the statutory requirement to pay off debt in a specific period is a foundation-stone of our system, and this belief has my full support. Where we come back to dubiety in our principles is that on examination, the loan sanction periods prove to be little more than conventions, useful conventions no doubt, but little more. They purport to be related to the life of the asset, but if anyone thinks that we can renew our stock of schools every 40 years, or even our houses every 60 years, and even more so, our sewers every 30 years, then he is, I fear, out of touch with reality. All that we can claim is that, by and large, repayment on this kind of basis is a reasonable and conventional practice.

Where the convention breaks down somewhat is in the practice of giving loan sanctions for equipment on a 15-year basis. When we build a school all the equipment, down to the last cup and saucer or micrometer screw-gauge, is part of the capital cost, and though the cup may be broken on the opening day, and the micrometer disappear during the first term, the replacement of that cup or gauge is revenue expenditure. It is part of the cost of maintaining the asset in its original form and the asset should in theory be so maintained for the whole of its life. Therefore to my mind, to give a short loan period for equipment and a long one for the building is in fact to throw doubt on the validity of the relationship between sanction periods and the lives of the assets. But in practice, I do not really dissent from this procedure. I merely use it to illustrate my theme that we are stronger on practice than on principle. In fact, there is a separate conventional practice in the education service, that in a new school or college, all items costing less than £2 are financed from revenue account.

We cannot therefore borrow money to buy an asset without superior sanction, and we must charge our revenue accounts with the cost of maintaining the asset and of interest, and of repaying the debt over a conventionally agreed period.

Methods of debt repayment

These paragraphs dealing with our methods of setting aside sums for debt repayment are mainly for the record, but do illustrate some of the fascinating practical problems involved. I mention the Consolidated Loans Fund (CLF), a very subtle and efficient piece of administrative machinery.

We have a choice about the manner in which we set aside sums for the liquidation of our debt. We are not here concerned with the series of transactions between ourselves as borrowers and the actual lenders of money. We are considering how we must charge the ratepayers through our revenue accounts each year a sum which will write off the debt over the loan sanction periods. The actual borrowing transactions are dealt with later.

First, quite simply, we may liquidate the debt by equal annual instalments of principal; this means that to provide for the repayment of £10,000 over 10 years, we would pay off £1,000 a year. In addition, we should have to pay from revenue account interest on the outstanding balance, so that our annual debt charges consist of £1,000 capital repayment each year plus a diminishing sum for interest. This method of repayment therefore starts with a high charge which reduces over the life of the loan as the interest element falls with the declining balance of debt. We like this method because as an asset ages its maintenance costs rise, and this is broadly offset by the annual decline in debt charges.

Alternatively, we can use a rather curious technique, known as the Notional Accumulating Sinking Fund. Under this method we set aside each year a sum of money which, if it were invested to yield $x\%$ per annum would produce the total capital sum required by the end of the period. Because we are not in fact setting aside the sum and investing it at the rate of $x\%$, we are required to include with the annual provision the sum which would have been earned by the earlier provisions if they had been invested. This you may find a curious conception. The advantage of it is that although the provision for repayment would start, in our example, with below £1,000, and would increase over the period (because the notional annual earnings would increase) to a figure higher than £1,000, this rise would tend to be offset by the decline in the other interest element, that is, the interest which has to be paid on the outstanding balance.

On the equal annual charge basis, the combined annual cost of repayment plus interest starts high and finishes low, but with the notional accumulating sinking fund, it tends to start low and finish high. But there are two significant points; the first is that the nearer the assumed rate of accumulation of the sinking fund is to the actual rate of interest paid on the outstanding balance, the nearer the annual charge comes to a stabilized charge over the whole life of the loan. Given that the two rates of interest, the notional and the actual, are the same, then we reach a perfect annuity, and the line for repayment, illustrated graphically, is horizontal as compared with a line which slopes up or down over the period of repayment.

The second significant point is that because less is paid off in the earlier years of a sinking fund of this type, the overall cost of interest is higher than under the first simple system.

There are some services in which a flat-rate annual charge for repayment and interest combined, or a combined charge which at least shows relatively little variation between first and final years, better suits the nature of the service, even though over the life of the loan the total charge is somewhat greater.

The tables in Appendix 2 illustrate those differences. There is room for difference of opinion about the appropriate method to use in particular situations. Personally I favour the system which pays off debt more quickly, and therefore costs less overall in interest, but there are those who urge that if by using the sinking fund method we slow down repayment, then when we take inflation into account we find that we are repaying our debt in less valuable pounds than those in which we incurred the debt. Is this a sound or a dubious argument? Who really bears the cost of inflation?

Our critics often allege that though our provision for repayment of debt over the conventionally assumed life of the asset is in practice sound enough, our method of financing the capital expenditure initially by borrowing for less than this period is less sound.

While we may be given 40 years in which to provide from revenue the wherewithal to pay off the debt incurred on the provision of a building, we do not in fact have to borrow for a 40-year period initially. Indeed we very seldom do. As you will observe from our advertisements in the press, we may borrow for very short periods, usually say, on average about 5 years, but very frequently for 7 days, and indeed on occasion, overnight only. Our critics say that we are borrowing short and investing long and that this is a grave weakness in the system. This system may indeed be theoretically weak, but in practice we have more than a century of experience to show that it is thoroughly workable. In other words, we are doing what the building societies do; only in theory could they expect to cash in all their assets to meet a shortage of lenders. We are really banking on the assumption that loan money will always be available—at a price—and that if it does dry up, then we will levy a rate to meet the shortage. This however, is something which we would never contemplate as being within the bounds of possibility.

If we simplify the picture by assuming that we borrow initially for 5 years to finance capital expenditure for which repayment provision will be made over 40 years, then at the end of 5 years we have to repay a loan for the full debt and re-borrow. We do not need to reborrow the whole of the initial outlay because by the end of the 5th year, if we assume that we have been making repayment provision by equal annual instalments of principal, we have set aside 5/40ths of the total provision for repayment, and therefore after 5 years we need to borrow only 35/40ths of the sum. This process goes on throughout the life of the loan sanction, so that again in theory, when we reach our 40th year having set aside 40/40ths we can then relieve ourselves entirely of the debt.

What is said above is something of an over-simplification because except in smaller authorities with little capital expenditure we cannot tolerate this detailed linking of actual borrowings with loan sanction periods. What we do in effect is to use the Consolidated Loans Fund, a system which has evolved from an earlier device, the mortgage loans pool. The CLF is a sophisticated technique.

The basic principle of the CLF is that the raising of capital funds is divorced from the use of those funds for capital expenditure. For purposes of the spending department the CLF becomes the lender to the borrowing account and the spending department complies with the statutory requirements for repayment. For purposes of the loan raising function the CLF borrows from the market on whatever terms are thought to be most advantageous. Into the Loans Fund we pour all our borrowings, irrespective of the period for which they are borrowed, and from the Loans Fund we make advances of capital funds to our spending committees to cover their capital expenditure. These spending committees pay their annual revenue provision for repayment of the debt into the CLF in compliance with the sanction requirements, and we repay any debt which becomes due to lenders from the CLF. This simplifies our problems considerably, yet beneath it all we are in fact reconciling, in our roundabout way, repeated short borrowings with longer loan sanction periods as described in the simplified example above.

If the amounts of repayment provision in the CLF available

from the spending committees are insufficient to meet repayments due to lenders, then we have more borrowing to do. If on the other hand the loans falling due at any one time are less than the amounts being provided by spending committees for their annual repayments, then we have a balance which we can use for new capital expenditure instead of reborrowing, but of course, those committees incurring the new capital expenditure have to make provision in the ordinary way for its repayment into the CLF over the sanction period. Usually, with the expanding capital programmes which most of us have, the annual repayment provisions, even though they are more than sufficient to meet the loans falling due for repayment in any given year, need to be supplemented by new borrowing to meet the new capital outlay.

A CLF therefore absorbs loans for all sorts of periods, and at a variety of interest rates. The interest which the CLF has to pay to lenders is also recharged to the departments who have borrowed from it; this is charged to borrowing departments at the average rate of all borrowings from the public by the CLF. A spending department therefore pays a rate of interest which varies from year to year as the CLF average rate varies.

This practice raises problems in a period of changing interest levels. The first problem is that we have to recognize that at any one time some services may be subsidizing others. If today our major outlay is on housing, and as at present the current borrowing rate is well above the CLF average, then the Housing Revenue Account is getting its new money cheaper than it would do if it was a separate borrower, and some of the current cost is being borne by other departments who though they still have old debts, may have no current capital outlay, and therefore no current borrowing at all.

But this leads us to the second problem which is indeed the answer to our first. There may well be times—one may be coming soon—when the average of the CLF will be higher than the current borrowing rate. Then the big current spenders may complain that by paying the CLF rate they are paying more than they need and are thus subsidizing the earlier borrowings of other committees.

Although on the interest side a CLF is obviously a 'swings and roundabouts' device, the larger authorities could not manage without it.

Methods of borrowing

In the last 7 or 8 years there has been a quiet but nevertheless thorough-going revolution in the techniques of local authority borrowing. Before the second world war the main methods of finance of capital expenditure were by local authority mortgages with the occasional stock issue by the larger authorities. In addition, a few authorities issued 3-month money bills. Others used, to a minor extent, a form of borrowing known as the 'housing bond' (specifically for the finance of housing capital expenditure) and there were a few authorities who regularly borrowed very short money in a small way. The government organization known as Public Works Loan Board was available to a few of the smaller local authorities.

During and after the war, the Public Works Loan Board was made available to all authorities, though we were left with the discretion to borrow small amounts locally if we wished.

(1) *Temporary borrowing*

The revolution really began when in 1953 the facilities of the Public Works Loan Board were suddenly withdrawn and local authorities were thrown on to the discipline of the market. The PWLB remained as lender of last resort to which access was extremely difficult, the rates charged being those which the PWLB regarded as current market rates.

This withdrawal of PWLB facilities coincided with a period of rising interest rates so that the first real step in the revolution was an extension of the borrowing by local authorities of very short funds, i.e. for an initial period of less than a year and for which a simple receipt sufficed. This was called 'temporary' borrowing because it was at one time considered only suitable for emergency use. It has theoretically less security than other borrowing, but until August 1967, it had the advantage to the local authority that being temporary, it did not bear stamp duty.

While it could be borrowed for up to 364 days, the normal period was 7 days or perhaps for 1 month and then at 7 days' notice.

With the exception of a few of the bolder treasurers, most treasurers had in the past only used temporary borrowing for very special purposes, such as to tide over between the expenditure and the receipt of a grant or for a month or two in anticipation of a stock issue. But as interest rates rose, and as the more daring authorities took more and more of their debt on a temporary basis, the general body of treasurers shed their timidity and the volume of temporary debt grew. At one stage we began to call such loans 'deposit loans' but recently we have returned to the original name.

It came in great variety, mainly on 7 days' notice or 1 month and thereafter at 7 days' notice, but 3-monthly, 6-monthly and 364-day loans became common; indeed, 2-day and overnight money was often used. Several quite critical financial periods were surmounted without difficulty and this gave added confidence to the treasurers working in this market. Because local authorities offered slightly more than Treasury bill or bank deposit rates, they began to attract commercial and industrial funds and indeed, institutional funds generally, which otherwise would have lain in the bank or been invested in Treasury bills, and money which came in on 7 days' notice often stayed for months or even years. We can say in all truth that, being thrown on to the market at a difficult time, treasurers established for themselves a new market in this temporary borrowing, assisted by a few energetic London brokers who served to bring together the potential lenders and the local authority borrowers. Though the development, once it started, was quite rapid, municipal treasurers did not rush into this field light-heartedly; many long and earnest arguments took place in our organized groups about the quantity of temporary debt which might safely be held, and various rules of thumb were evolved. Despite all this, more and more money was borrowed on this basis until by 1962 local authority temporary debt amounted to more than £1,000m. The Radcliffe Committee saw the danger of this and as early as 1959 had reported that local authorities 'have been piling up short-term debt in a way that is clearly contrary to the funding policy of the monetary authorities'.

In 1963 the Treasury decided to call a halt; in consultation with a group of municipal treasurers, they set about devising means whereby a proper control could be established on temporary borrowing by local authorities. The Treasury were not free from embarrassment in proposing to introduce control. As they had not told local authorities that they must submit to discipline of the market, they could not therefore complain when local authorities exercised their daring and ingenuity and developed a new market even though this new market did not entirely suit the Treasury's book. The treasurers did not fail to make this point.

But of course the issue went deeper than this. Because of the effect of temporary borrowing on bank deposits and on the sale of Treasury bills, the whole of the national economy was feeling the effect of this new form of borrowing by local authorities; most treasurers were themselves beginning to feel that events had gone far enough. The occasional crises became increasingly serious and a good deal of 'hot' money was thought to be involved.

The agreement reached seemed at the time, and indeed still does, to be a very fair one. Local authorities agreed to accept a restriction on borrowing which was initially for a period of less than a year, to 20% of their total debt. Three-quarters of this temporary debt could be for periods of up to three months and the other quarter could extend to 364 days. This was surely an eminently generous arrangement bearing in mind that it did not affect debt initially borrowed for longer periods than a year, but which was within the last year of its life.

(2) *Public Works Loan Board*

But the local authority representatives did not accept this restriction without a struggle and extracted from the Treasury a number of concessions, the most important of which was that the Public Works Loan Board would be opened again to local authorities for up to 50% of their long-term borrowing each year, at the current government borrowing rate plus a small management charge, and not at the normal market rate for local authority borrowing; at that time this gave an interest advantage of between $\frac{3}{4}$ and 1% for PWLB money, though today the margin is very much smaller. The Treasury could not undertake to open the Public Works Loan Board door so widely all at once, but tentatively promised a 20% access in the first year to be extended, unless circumstances proved too unfavourable, to 50% over 4 years. At the same time because quite a large number of local authorities had far more than 20% of their debt on a temporary basis, they too were given 4 years in which to fund the excess over the new datum line. All these arrangements were enshrined in a White Paper on Local Authority Borrowing in October 1963.

Unfortunately, this was a best laid scheme which went agley. Access to PWLB was for the given quota of all long-term borrowing in the year, and not merely for borrowing to cover new capital expenditure. This meant that renewals of loans ranked for PWLB quota so that the quicker the turnover of our market borrowing, the quicker we could establish a large sum under the PWLB quota. This realization coincided with a period in which interest rates were still very high so that treasurers in any event would have been inclined to borrow as short as possible. The outcome of this situation was that treasurers tended to take their PWLB quota for 10 years, the minimum period for which the board would lend, and to make their market borrowings as short as possible.

This, along with increasing capital expenditure, led to demands on the PWLB far in excess of those which they had expected. The outcome was that while for the second year the quota rate was raised to 30%, for the third year it was retained at this amount instead of being increased generally to 40% though, shortly afterwards, the 40% was allowed to certain of what were regarded as the less prosperous parts of the country.

At the same time, in order to combat the growth of a form of loan which had emerged specifically to allow authorities to turn over their market borrowing quickly, that is to say, borrowing for one year—a day longer than temporary loans—subject to one month's notice after 11 months, the Treasury made a rule that quota would not be allowed on the replacement or renewal of borrowings for which a quota had been earned in the previous financial year.

This slowed the rate of access to the PWLB but not as much as was required and at the end of the third year, by which stage under the original plan we should have reached 50%, the 30/40% quota was retained.

From the 1 April 1967 an even more important change has also been made; the PWLB quota no longer applies to the renewal of loans, but is calculated as a percentage of new capital payments, whether or not the capital outlay is actually financed by borrowing. The quotas have been adjusted to 34% and 44% to partially offset this restriction.

The full implications of this change have by no means been properly assimilated by local authorities. We had no choice but to accept it because the Chancellor made it clear that the amount of money available to local authorities from the PWLB was distinctly limited and much below what the local authorities would have liked.

In his budget speech the Chancellor made an oblique remark that the time had perhaps come when the provision of substantial capital sums for local authorities through the PWLB in the present way should again be reviewed. We are by no means clear what he had in mind.

There are many of us who feel that the financing of the PWLB as part of the Consolidated Fund and from the budget surplus is itself illogical. There seems to be no reason why advances from PWLB to local authorities should be raised from taxation, so that there is no need to regard it as part of the national budget. If all that the Chancellor means is that he will finance the PWLB by direct government borrowings, then we shall look forward with interest to the details of the scheme, but we fear that he has something more sinister in mind; we await disclosure of his intentions with disquiet[1].

(3) *Mortgages and bonds*

Without exaggeration the bond which has come into use as a major borrowing instrument in recent years can be claimed as the outcome of an exercise in form design. The process began in Manchester about ten years ago in efforts to simplify the rather terrifying appearance of the mortgage deed used to acknowledge a loan. Difficult to complete and to understand, this was loaded with signatures and had an unnecessary seal of magnificent proportions.

A mortgage deed is of course a document of great historical significance and, despite its age, it is a fundamental instrument in modern communal life. The local authority mortgage originally did actually mortgage local authority property against a loan, though for many years (since 1933 in general and earlier under various private Acts) what we have been mortgaging are the rates and revenues of the authority which are the direct security for all our loans (except for temporary borrowing, though the security even here is in effect the same).

Over the course of 4 or 5 years, as a result of successive efforts in form design, the document was reduced from a sheet more than twice foolscap size to quarto; it was drastically simplified in layout. It followed the layout of a modern insurance policy, the number of signatures was reduced and those which remained were printed in facsimile. Even the seal was printed onto the form instead of being embossed.

During these procedures for simplification we had managed to persuade the Inland Revenue that we should follow cheque

[1] We now know that the Chancellor had this simple and logical course in mind and proposes to establish a National Loans Fund for the purpose.

procedure for the payment of duty and we were thus enabled to do away with the embossing of duty stamps on the deed, and replace them by a slogan to say that duty was being accounted for in bulk. Though there were strong areas of resistance, the simplified mortgage began to be adopted rapidly by local authorities.

Having thus progressively cut down the mortgage to size, there emerged a more ready acceptance of the truth that this was only a piece of paper acknowledging a debt and that the idea of mortgaging either the properties or the revenues of the authority was, like the seal, a relic of the middle ages. The bond was then the natural outcome.

I have stressed the background to the evolution of the bond, because it is a clear indication—of great importance to the practical administrator—of the benefits which can derive from the analysis of purpose and the clear thinking which the pursuit of form design necessitates. This is particularly significant in this case because the bond has led to a substantial clarification of local authority borrowing practices generally.

The local bond is a simplified borrowing instrument—an ideal borrowing instrument, we should like to think—devised after the deliberate analysis of a variety of borrowing instruments—to which we naturally turned once we had rationalized the mortgage as far as possible. This analysis led to the evolution of a new instrument which we decided to call a bond, and which contained all the benefits and, we hoped, none of the drawbacks of the existing instruments. This conception was put to the Treasury who welcomed it with open arms to the extent that they went to the trouble of persuading a private member of Parliament to introduce, under the private members' bill procedure, a short Act of Parliament giving all local authorities power to use this new bond. (The Act also included a few other improvements in local authority financial procedures).

The bond is now a simple acknowledgement of debt, but its security is exactly the same as that of the mortgage. Another of the apparent oddities of local authority methods which work well enough in practice, is that while a lender is technically buying a bond, what he gets is not a bond, but a certificate of registration which shows that he is registered as the holder of a bond in our books. The bond is therefore intangible—in a very true sense, our word is our bond—and in this the bond is in fact identical with stock. What you receive when you buy stock is a stock certificate certifying that you are the owner of some stock, but as for the stock itself, seek it as you will, you will not find it. This simplified bond can now be issued practically instantaneously over the counter or by return of post, for an investment, and there are many subsidiary procedures which have been either abolished or streamlined as a result of it—for example, it bears only one (lithographed) signature, and it does not even carry the imitation seal which appears on the mortgage. We have long ceased to send it by registered mail.

I must admit with some puzzlement and a good deal of regret that although there has been rapid adoption of the bond, there are still many authorities who have as yet failed to grasp the significance of this new opportunity for streamlining their borrowing procedure.

We know disappointingly little about the sources of our investors in bonds—formerly in mortgages. There was a time when fairly detailed records were kept by the larger authorities, but they did not serve any very practical purpose and have on the whole been abandoned. Certainly in the old days, and even between the wars, a great deal of money came from local people and local authorities frequently accepted sums as small as £50, perhaps as offering something like a savings club to local people.

But since the war, even your small investor is becoming much more sophisticated and follows the interest rates more closely. Money no longer goes to the local town hall; it seeks the best rates and fringe conditions. Administration costs have become more of a worry; the cost of handling small investments (for which in any event there are now many other channels) is too high and many local authorities will now take sums of only £500 or more.

The small investor is still a fractionally cheaper source judged by interest levels, yet most of our money comes from institutions and some authorities borrow from institutions only in minimum sums of £50,000 claiming with some justice that the slightly higher interest rates are offset by cheaper administration.

(4) *The negotiable bond*

But one outcome of the bond which surprised not only the Treasury and the Bank of England, but the designers of the bond themselves, was the almost simultaneous evolution of the bond in a negotiable form. This negotiable type of bond was conceived by Warburgs, the merchant bankers, in collaboration with Manchester.

A mortgage or an over-the-counter 'tap' bond is marketable in the sense that a stockbroker will usually find a client for it if the holder wishes to sell it, but there is no 'market' in the sense that daily buying and selling rates are quoted on the stock exchange or elsewhere. In its truly negotiable form, the bond requires essentially the making of arrangements whereby a bond can be transferred within the same day in London and its advantages are that this instant negotiability produces, or should produce, a saving in the interest rate of about $\frac{1}{2}\%$.

The original intention was that these bonds should be issued through the discount market which, as you know, is that section of the London market most interested in very short 'paper', and this in fact, is what happened. But the stock exchange very rapidly saw that unless they adapted themselves to this new situation, they might be losing a good deal of business; consequently stock exchange regulations for the issue of local authority stock were rapidly modified and the stock exchange became handlers of local authority bond issues in the same way as the merchant bankers and the discount market.

Originally, there were hopes that there would be issues of local authority negotiable bonds each week, but the state of the market has not permitted this and the Bank of England (whose consent is needed to any issue of this negotiable paper under the Control of Borrowing Order) have been extremely cautious—though perhaps still not cautious enough—in the way in which bonds have been released, and a queue has been formed of local authorities wishing to make an issue. The limit for any local authority is £1m.[1] At the same time, although the Bank accept the bond as a satisfactory borrowing instrument, they have refused to accept it for overnight collateral, and this has very substantially reduced its value to the market, and in particular to the discount houses. The upshot of this restriction has been that the market has become far more quickly clogged with this form of borrowing than we expected when it was first launched, and partly as a result of this clogging and partly because local authorities have been over-anxious to pick up this form of borrowing which gave them something like $\frac{1}{2}\%$ below the current over-the-counter bond rate, interest rates have gradually moved against local authorities until a time was reached quite recently when we had the absurd situation that the negotiable bond rate was higher than that for the non-negotiable bond. The total sum now on issue is over £200m.

Why, you may ask, should treasurers go on issuing bonds of this kind with an adverse interest situation? A fair question, but the answer is not easy. The accusation has been made that the market has taken advantage of local authorities' eagerness to issue negotiable bonds and has gradually hardened the rate against us. But the market has replied, with some justice, that a hardening of the interest rate should have been a signal to local authorities that this form of paper was becoming indigestible. Local authorities on the other hand, while expressing anxiety at the way the interest rate was moving against them, were reluctant to refuse an opportunity of issuing negotiable bonds when their name came to the top of the list run by the Bank of England. We may perhaps also criticize the Bank for giving authorities an opportunity of issuing negotiable bonds when the market was over-filled with them, for refusing to

---

[1] This has been revised since this paper was prepared, on to a sliding scale related to total loan debt at 31 March each year with a maximum of £5m.

facilitate the market by accepting the bonds for overnight collateral and finally for giving consent to issues of bonds at rates which were clearly against the interest of local authorities.

However, we must admit that negotiable paper of this kind, which being for a minimum of a year is just outside the control on temporary borrowing, is a problem for the Bank and we must not be too critical if instead of opposing this unexpected new form of borrowing, they have tried to run a middle course.

The ball is now really with the local authorities; if the rates or conditions are unfavourable, then they should not borrow in this way. After all, the volume of money involved is relatively trifling.

But this should be made quite clear; negotiable bonds were not issued as a means of opening a new market for local authorities; they were issued only for the simple reason that we believed that this form of borrowing would be cheaper. As soon as the interest difference disappears, or becomes adverse, then there is no point in issuing local authority negotiable bonds. Some of the more determined treasurers have refused to borrow on negotiable bonds at rates equal to or above what they could borrow on non-negotiable bonds from the institutions.

Unless, therefore, there is some re-adjustment in the market, the local authority negotiable bond has reached the limit of its usefulness. Recently however, the negotiable bond rate has moved in our favour again.

Rather to our annoyance the London Market, enthusiastic as it was at first for the negotiable bond, insists on calling these instruments LAB's or Local Authority Bonds, seeming to think that this is the principal form in which local authorities borrow by bonds. In fact, as you will by now have gathered, local authorities are borrowing far more money by non-negotiable bonds, which we now call local bonds, and the negotiable bond is a minor activity. For clarity's sake we should adhere to the 'LANB' for local authority negotiable bonds and 'LB' for local bond, that is, the bond in its over-the-counter tap and less readily marketable form. This is indeed where its real future lies. There is a difficulty of nomenclature here because although we call our local bonds non-negotiable, they can in fact be sold through the stock exchange, though there is no regular 'market' for them.

Even if the negotiable bond (or yearling bond as it was originally nicknamed although issues are not necessarily confined to one year) has had less success than was originally hoped, it has brought an unexpected further clarification of the fundamental concepts of local authority borrowing.

The upshot of this development has been that it has emphasized the unity of the local authority borrowing instrument. The bond in its negotiable form was soon recognized as a stock issue for a period of a year, instead of from 10 to 15 years; a stock issue placed rather than offered to the public, but nevertheless a minor stock issue. At the same time a negotiable bond was by birth merely an ordinary over-the-counter bond for which special provision had been made for rapid transferability, mainly by the compounding for transfer of stamp duty and the use of a London agent.

Naive though this may now seem, this development shed a new light on local authority borrowing practices; we see now that we have a situation in which we can use the same document, a bond, for either over-the-counter borrowing on tap, or for issue as a negotiable bond, or for issue for what we now call stock, which is in fact merely bonds negotiable for a longer period.

We have not yet reached the end of this development, though another step was taken in the 1967 Budget. As part of the examination of this new borrowing instrument a detailed study was made of the two codes of duty applicable to local (and other) borrowing—the *ad valorem* stamp duty code, and the loan capital duty code. While these duties are basically for the same amount, curious inconsistencies and anomalies appear at various points where renewal or transfer of a document takes place. Local authorities pressed the Inland Revenue either for rationalization of these two codes or preferably for the abolition of stamp duty on local authority lending altogether. To our great satisfaction the more far-reaching proposal has been adopted, and in the 1967 Budget all stamp duties on local authority borrowing and transfers were abolished from August 1967. This gives us and our lenders a useful though not enormous saving in cash but more important still, it gives us an opportunity for further streamlining of our procedures. Indeed, we have not yet realized the full implications for improvement in administration and flexibility which this useful step offers us.

The Act of Parliament authorizing the issue of the new bond provided that regulations should be drawn up by the Treasury to cover the details of bond administration and a set of very simple regulations was produced. Although we have now proved that the bond covered by these regulations in its negotiable form is identical with a stock issue, there also exists a very complex and antique set of stock regulations, which has more pages than the set of bond regulations has paragraphs. What we now seek is an amalgamation into one code of the stock and the bond regulations in a form as simple, or nearly as simple, as those we have procured for the bond.

Perhaps you will say that this unity of the local authority borrowing instrument and the scope for simplification was apparent all the time and that recent recognition of these possibilities is nothing to boast about. But this is often the reaction to all good O & M ideas—it is so simple, why didn't we think about it before? This is not an easy question to answer except by saying that after all we are all only human, and leave it at that. We will certainly increase reluctance to change if we make too much of the point.

(5) *Money bills*

I mentioned earlier in this paper that some few authorities had made slight use in the inter-war years of borrowing on 3-month money bills. There has been quite recently an important development in this field.

There is no general power for local authorities to borrow by means of bills, but quite a number of authorities have over the years through local acts, obtained powers to issue 3-month money bills, subject to Treasury consent, for capital purposes.

Just what these instruments are is by no means clear. They are certainly in the same category as Treasury bills and they may be nearer to promissory notes than bills of exchange. Certainly they are bearer documents with the fullest and most easy negotiability. However, an exact nomenclature does not seem to be very significant because again, however shaky the theory may be, in practice everything goes very smoothly.

For reasons not now easy to see, but probably based on the caution of treasurers in times gone by against very short borrowing, money bills were not widely used except, like temporary borrowing, as bridging finance in anticipation of the issue of stock. Nevertheless some dozen authorities continued as a matter of policy to issue money bills regularly but their powers were limited to the raising of small amounts of either £½m or £1m except that Glasgow could deal in up to £2m worth of bills.

In recent years with a period of high interest rates, and after experience of the success of temporary borrowing, authorities began to show more interest in the use of their capital bill powers. To their chagrin, however, the Treasury and the Bank have refused to allow any more authorities to bring into use their bill powers, though those authorities who have kept up the practice for many years have been allowed to continue.

Manchester is one of the authorities who let its bill powers fall into disuse and who consequently were denied authority to revive these powers. However, in a recent local act we thought we would increase our general powers by seeking authority to issue money bills, not for capital purposes, but in anticipation of the receipt of revenue—i.e. another form of bridging finance. All local authorities have of course substantial sums of revenue owing to them, and are often forced to cover the gap between revenue expenditure and income by bank overdraft or temporary borrowing. We therefore included a clause asking for money bill powers for revenue as well as capital purposes, up to £5m. Apart from asking us to reduce the figure to £3m, the Treasury offered no objection to the clause and indicated to our surprise that their objection to the issue of capital purposes money bills did not extend to bills in anticipation of revenue.

The Treasury's explanation of their attitude was that the Bank's regulations for bills provide that for 60 days in the year continuously, or in two periods of 30 days, there must be no bills on issue and as these bills were 'self-financing' by the ultimate receipt of the revenue, they did not regard this as an overall increase in local authority borrowing.

Nevertheless, having revenue bill monies does help to bridge a gap which would normally be filled by overdraft or temporary borrowing, so that to this extent this kind of borrowing which is hardly distinguishable from capital borrowing reduces the need for other more expensive methods.

This facility allowed to Manchester could not be denied to other authorities and the Treasury readily conceded that any authority putting a local Act before Parliament could take similar powers for money bills in anticipation of revenue. They went further than this and agreed that instead of a round sum of £3m or some similar appropriate sum, local authorities could seek power to issue bills for up to 20% of their rate income in any year. In a subsequent parliamentary bill Manchester have adopted this 20% figure and this increases our scope from £3m to, at present, nearly £4½m. (Incidentally, we asked for and obtained power for 20% of rate intake or £3m, whichever was the greater—after all, one never knows what might happen to rates!)

Several large authorities have already received similar powers and a brisk market in local authority 3-month bills, very acceptable to the discount houses, is now in being. What is very gratifying is that while there was only a small amount of LA bills on the market, the rate was the same as that for fine bank bills; now that we have larger sums to offer the market is prepared to take a rate roughly between Treasury bill rate and that for fine bank bills—a very useful improvement.

What we regret is that the three biggest developments in local authority borrowing practices in recent years—the development of the temporary money market, the readily negotiable bond, and this new form of revenue bill, are all at the short end of the market. However, our new relations with the

Public Works Loan Board tend to lengthen our borrowing periods for longer-term debt so that these two factors have a balancing effect.

(6) *Stock*

Local authorities do still, of course, borrow by means of stock issues and we are hoping to bring this technique into closer relationship with our borrowing by bonds. However, except in those local authorities where the demand for capital is so great that they must seize every opportunity to borrow we are on the whole reluctant to use this method even when the opportunity is offered.

The Treasury and the Bank have made a rule that only authorities who can make an issue of at least £3m should be on their list and issues are few and far between. Over the last 3 years there have been only 26 issues covering £330m; if we exclude the 2 issues by GLC for £110m, the balance is not really a very significant sum.

Our objections are of course that, with interest rates high, we are reluctant to borrow for the periods for which stock is normally issued. Moreover, I think I can say that we are becoming uneasy about the cost of borrowing by stock and that we do not feel that the coupon rate which attaches to stock fully takes into account the cost of issue and the negotiability of this form of paper. There is a sort of mystique about stock issues of which the more hard-headed treasurers are becoming increasingly sceptical.

The demand for stock in the quantities we usually issue is confined to a relatively small institutional market and this puts us at something of a disadvantage. In particular we are uneasy about the inter-relationship of those who do most of the underwriting and most of the buying. This is something we are having a close look at.

Incidentally, we have not made up our minds what we mean by a 'successful' issue; if it is heavily oversubscribed, the brokers say it was a success, but the treasurer whose local authority has issued it, tends to think that this oversubscription means that the rate offered must have been too generous. *Per contra*, if most of it is left with the underwriters, the market call it a failure, but the treasurer concerned takes some satisfaction that with the help of the underwriters he has obtained his money at a rate lower than the market really thought adequate. However, I suppose we ought to admit that under- or oversubscription often arises from market changes between the days when the terms are fixed and the issue made.

What we need is a new look at local authority stock issues as penetrating and as fruitful as that which has been given to the mortgage.

Borrowing versus pay-as-you-go

There is one subject of constant controversy in the field of local authority capital finance on which the reactions of the economists would be helpful to treasurers. This is the question of how far we should borrow to cover our capital expenditure and how far we should pay as we go. Linked with this is the question whether, when we do borrow, we should keep our loan repayment periods as short as possible. The joker in the pack in this game is called 'inflation'.

Local authorities bear a good deal of capital expenditure directly from revenue in a somewhat happy-go-lucky way, e.g. if the Police department is to renew 12 motor cars every year, after a life of say 3 years, then there is obviously no point in incurring capital expenditure on these cars even though, by any definition, they can be regarded as capital assets. This applies to several of our services where we have regular renewals of vehicles or equipment.

In addition, however, to the provision of a good deal of capital equipment rather casually from revenue account, many local authorities have a more specific policy of levying a capital purposes rate (CPR)—in Manchester at the moment this is 6*d*. in the £—which is used for the purpose of providing capital assets without borrowing. Similarly many authorities have exercised a general power to establish what are called Capital

97

Funds, that is to say a fund into which revenue monies can be paid either by rate levy or by the setting aside of some *ad hoc* revenues. If I may quote Manchester again, we have a capital fund which is fed not by a direct levy but by the income we receive from our investments in the Ship Canal Company, originally made in 1891 and now free from any commitment on our part so that the income from this investment now represents a clear profit to us. This 'free' income could otherwise be used to reduce the rate levy.

We support the policy of pay-as-you-go on the grounds that it saves interest charges with the result that all that we collect from the ratepayer is ploughed back into new capital assets instead of being used substantially for the payment of interest to lenders. This is all very well as far as it goes, but there are those treasurers who argue that by making present ratepayers finance capital expenditure for the provision of assets which will be used by future generations, we are wrongly taxing the current generation of ratepayers, and that this levy for capital purposes, instead of being used by us to save interest charges on the rate, should be left to 'fructify in the pockets of the ratepayer', to use a well-worn phrase.

I have always been a staunch believer in pay-as-you-go— maybe because I was brought up in this way—and I am sure that for regular purchases of assets such as the motor car, as already mentioned, this is undoubtedly the thing to do. Manchester's total capital expenditure in each year is at present about £30m, and our debt charges consisting of provision for annual repayment and interest on the outstanding debt are about £15m. Both these figures have risen sharply in recent years, and one wonders at what point the annual provision for repayment of debt and interest on outstanding debt will be equivalent to our new annual capital expenditure.

We have already reached a point in our provision of a 6*d*. rate for capital purposes where the interest and debt charges which we would have been bearing on the assets purchased from our CPR, if we had not had such a policy for a number of years, would have been greater than the product of the 6*d*. rate.

We can therefore argue that from this point onwards our capital purposes rate policy represents a definite saving to the present ratepayers through, in a sense, the generosity of past generations of ratepayers.

We may take it that however logical it might be to argue that this policy should have applied to the whole of capital expenditure, the amount of capital expenditure in the early years was such that we could not conceivably have launched this project on the ratepayer.

But recently, while I still adhere to this middle course, more and more doubt has been entering my mind as to the absolute logicality of the argument of avoiding capital borrowing as far as possible and paying off debt as quickly as possible when money has to be borrowed. The problem is raised of course, by inflationary trends. We could well argue that if we borrow £1,000 now and repay it over 10 years, then the cost of that £1,000 even when adding interest on the outstanding debt throughout the period, is less in real terms than the cost of £1,000 spent today.

The issue depends of course on the rates of interest payable on debt and the rate at which the value of money falls, and we have done a number of calculations with the help of our computer to show where the break-even point occurs.

This matter in fact becomes too complicated for my purely practical approach. £1,000 has to be laid out initially, so that £1,000 worth of resources is consumed and all we are arguing about is whether or not the ratepayers as ratepayers should bear this immediately, or whether they should attempt to push some of the cost of this on to lenders by borrowing money from them and repaying them in a devalued currency. If the borrower gains by delaying repayment, then the lender loses a like amount.

Attempts to reach finality on this point are bedevilled by the fact that there will never be an end to capital expenditure by local authorities. There seems to be an impression in the minds of every generation of councillors, that once we have surmounted the present problems, then matters will settle down, but no matter how hard we have tried in the past we cannot keep pace with the need for new capital development. However much we have spent, the need to spend even more in future has been clear. Of course, the arrears brought about by two world wars are not without their significance. I am quite clear in my mind that by the time we have rid ourselves of all the old buildings which we now consider to be a burden to us (some of which are 100 years old), we shall need to be replacing those which we built in the early years of our redeveloping period and are building now. We shall, for example, need another 10 to 15 years before we have provided sufficient houses to meet our needs as we now see them, and by that time our first houses will be over 60 years old and of very unacceptable quality; the cycle will start again but on a bigger and better standard.

This being so, arguments about slowing down the rate of provision for the repayment of debt based on the devaluation of money seem unrealistic. While they might be true if we were reaching the end of our capital outlay, they cannot be true if we accept that a heavy capital programme is with us indefinitely. There is also the point of view that our successors may not like the assets of the debt with which we are saddling them.

The distinction between the policy of pay-as-you-go (a rate levied for capital purposes) and the use of capital funds is of some interest. Local authorities must in each year levy a 'sufficient' rate—that is, a rate sufficient to meet their properly estimated outgoings—and neither more nor less, except for marginal working balances. This means that we cannot carry forward any balance of rate indefinitely, but must put all balances to the credit of the next year's period of account. Following from this we cannot accumulate any underspending from the capital purposes rate but we must spend it up within the year. If, therefore, we have any balance of the CPR at the end of the year we must use this for expediting payment of debt or use it to reduce next year's rate levy.

But a capital fund is in a different category; here the law allows us to accumulate a balance and to carry it forward until needed. We have great elasticity with capital funds because either we can use them for paying capital expenditure on behalf of spending committees without loading them with a debt responsibility, or we can meet their expenditure subject to repayment of the debt over an appropriate period either with or without an interest charge. Our Manchester practice is to require spending committees to repay advances from the capital fund, with interest on the outstanding balance, and in this way we continue to build up the capital fund by accumulating the interest in it, because in fact we are not ourselves paying any interest on the money which feeds the capital fund.

If this seems a little hard on the ratepayers, we consider it at least to be sound long-term policy. While a capital purposes rate is normally used to finance small items of capital outlay and perhaps expenditure which is on the borderline between capital and revenue, there are no very clear ideas about whether there are any distinct purposes for which a capital fund should be used. To the borrowing committees, as long as repayment and interest are required, there is no practical difference between getting their needs from the capital fund or from borrowed money through the CLF. In Manchester we tend to use the capital fund for expenditures which have a considerable earning capacity so that the interest and repayment does not fall substantially on the ratepayers.

Incidentally, although underspendings on rate fund accounts on any year have to be carried forward to the next year, there is the interesting exception that the law does allow us to put these balances into a capital fund if we wish, and some authorities do just that. You may feel that the difference between a CPR and a capital fund is somewhat illusory; you could well be right, but in practice we find the distinction useful.

Centralized borrowing and the future of the PWLB

There are those both inside and outside local government who believe that the capital monies needed by the local authorities should be supplied at cost by the central government, just as the Exchequer supplies the capital needed by the nationalized industries. There are three arguments against this view; the money may on the whole be borrowed more easily if a large number of local authorities are individually seeking a large proportion of the capital which they need; local authorities resent measures which put them further under the control of Whitehall; and there is much to be said for those who spend the money having the problem of raising it.

Until recently the Treasury seemed to support at least the first of the reasons advanced above. During the discussions which led to the White Paper on Local Authority Borrowing they put forward the view that they chose to take advantage of the ingenuity of treasurers and their finance committees for the raising of considerable capital sums.

The Treasury's view now is less clear, because of the reference which, in his 1967 budget speech, the Chancellor made about the need to look again at the way in which funds have been supplied by the PWLB to local authorities. If he simply meant that the PWLB should be divorced from the Consolidated Fund and that funds should be raised in the market specifically by the Exchequer for lending on to local authorities, then this would be very much a step in the right direction. If, on the other hand, he meant that the whole of the funds of local authorities should be supplied centrally, or if, as is just conceivable, he meant that on the contrary, the PWLB doors should again be closed against local authorities, then this would cause us considerable concern. Let us hope that he meant merely the separation of PWLB financing from the budget; we would all be much in favour of this.[1] If we can obtain half of our funds from the PWLB then that is as far as we should go. After all, rates and government grants each bear about the same amount of local expenditure and this form of compromise seems typical of our national outlook and none the worse for that.

Those local authorities who find the raising of funds burdensome—and these are mainly either the very large or the very

---

[1] As shown earlier, he did mean this, but during the debate the Financial Secretary to the Treasury supported the view that all local authority capital should in due course be supplied by the Exchequer.

small authorities—have strongly urged that local authorities should set up their own central borrowing organization; there could be a place for this providing it was an alternative to the local raising of funds and not intended to replace the activities of individual local authorities entirely. A great deal would depend on how such a system would be organized.

But when under pressure from the Treasury during our discussions on local authority borrowing, we threatened to consider setting up our own borrowing agency, the Treasury made very clear—with good reason—that if the local authorities set up an agency which was likely to borrow between £500m and £750m a year they, the Treasury, would have to exercise just as much control over this as if the organization was part of the Exchequer's financing. After all, the nationalized boards were originally charged with raising their own capital funds, but their needs were so great—and unsupported by a truly local market—that the Exchequer considered that there would be less disruptive effect if these funds were provided by the Exchequer.

Capital planning

Capital forecasting or the planning of capital expenditure over a number of years ahead may seem a clear necessity but is more difficult than the outsider might imagine; nevertheless some very earnest attempts are being made by the local governments and by Whitehall to develop capital planning and programming for local authorities.

The danger of meeting the cost of assets from borrowed money is that the ratepayers, and more importantly the members who represent them, only feel the immediate burden of the interest and the annual repayment charges (and of course the cost of running the asset created); by financing from loan monies they are relieved of the necessity of having to provide the whole of the capital sum in the year in which the expenditure is incurred. This encourages a tendency to regard capital expenditure perhaps rather more light-heartedly than is proper;

after all 'only 7s. 9d. a week' provides a great temptation to the buying of a washing machine, or what have you. Treasurers never cease from impressing upon their councils that the time for the control of revenue expenditure begins when a capital scheme is first proposed.

In recent years, therefore, more and more local authorities have been producing three- or five-year comprehensive programmes of capital expenditure and the size of these programmes is quite properly causing considerable alarm both to the local authorities involved and to the government. Government ministries have been calling in recent years for even longer capital programmes on such services as health and highways. Educational building programmes have been closely controlled and built into long-term forecasts for many years. There has, however, been the danger that individual ministries have looked at their own services without these programmes having been built into a co-ordinated whole. More attention is now being given to this problem and the need for comprehensive inter-departmental programmes is being more fully recognized, particularly as local authority expenditure on capital account is impinging more and more on the national economy.

One of our major difficulties in capital planning arises oddly enough from excessive and unenlightened interference from government departments. We may readily admit that the local authority sector must submit to overall control of investment, but need we to be told that we should build a health clinic rather than an old people's home?

Loan sanction procedure, introduced in the days of primitive local government, is being used excessively for detailed policy control. We try locally to plan our overall capital investment and perhaps to impose a ration on ourselves. Then we try to determine our own priorities within this plan. When we then seek loan sanction for say, our old people's home, we are told that the government's allocation of sanctions for this purpose is exhausted, but that they have a ration available for a health centre—which is perhaps lower on our lists of priorities—if we care to apply for it. This is highly frustrating. We accept without question that some omniscient overlord should decide how much the local authority capital investment should be for the year and we will even accept that someone in Whitehall shall have the power to allocate this to local authorities on the basis of a case stated as to need. But who is more competent than ourselves to decide whether the needs of our area are greater for old people's welfare than for health, to take two services quite at random?

What is doubly aggravating is to find government departments—especially the Ministry of Transport—coming to us towards the end of the year with the story that they have some capital allocation to spare, and can we produce a road scheme —however low in priority—which can be started before the year's end? The final irony is of course that these 'allocations' are not of cash, but simply of permission to spend our own money, though some grant is often involved with road schemes.

Things are getting better, and comprehensive planning, and greater co-ordination at Whitehall, will bring further improvements. We hope that if as a result of the activities of the Royal Commission on Local Government we are reorganized into larger areas, greater flexibility within overall allocations will be possible.

Another of the problems confronting would-be long term capital planners is the disruptive effect of stop-go policies. In the larger authorities, any scheme is likely to take several years to reach the starting line and once started, it can scarcely be halted except disastrously. Yet too often in recent years we have been expected to apply first the brake, and then the accelerator, in ways which do not do the engine any good.

Before a local authority capital scheme reaches the stage of being included in a capital programme, it has been through a great many trials and tribulations and careful examinations, so that the schemes which reach the stage of inclusion in a provisional programme have been very thoroughly scrutinized, and are supported by a very good case indeed. If the net result of the combination of all these tested schemes is therefore to produce a demand for a sum of money which is frightening to the council, there is considerable difficulty in deciding which parts of the programme can be taken out. Among other things a good deal of our capital expenditure is inter-related. There is no point, for example, in clearing slums and redeveloping a large clearance area if, as well as houses, we do not also provide schools, clinics, roads, swimming-baths and libraries and the rest of the community services, to say nothing of the shopping centres.

Moreover, there are important items of expenditure which will not wait; a great deal of the capital outlay on absolute basic services in local government is on the renewal of assets, many of which are now 75 to 100 years old. There are major sewers for example, in Manchester, which are very nearly 100 years old, and the abattoir which we have just replaced was in fact more than 100 years old. We have swimming-baths still in use, as the chairman of the Baths Committee likes to remind us, which were built before Lincoln freed the slaves. As a result of slum clearance and redevelopment many of our present assets are not only obsolete but in the wrong places. We are now expected to produce clean air, and equally we are told that our rivers must be cleansed, but clean air costs a good deal of money initially, and our rivers will only be cleansed if very many out-moded sewage disposal works are completely rebuilt at vast expense, and if industry will do something positive about its effluents. While we cannot have good local services without thriving commerce and industry, we cannot have thriving commerce and industry without good local services, roads, sewers, adequate open spaces and a healthy and well-educated population.

In recent times economists in general and Treasury ministers in particular have been inclined to repeat as an article of holy writ that public investment must be slowed down to allow private investment to develop. They may be right but where do we draw the line? There is no point in providing factories without roads and sewers to serve them and an adequate police and fire service. Factories will not operate properly unless we have arranged a good supply of wholesome water for them.

I spent a good deal of my early youth in a Northumbrian mining village where almost all the houses, and such public services as there were, had been provided by the colliery company. This was not out of kindness of heart, but because the mines could not be run without labour, and labour has to be housed. Must we not then as local authorities provide housing as part of industry? Where does industrial development end? And nowadays, has not labour to be healthy and reasonably well educated? So where do we draw the line? The answer is presumably, to use a well-worn phrase, that we must strike a balance, but we must not talk as though public investment is a luxury.

At many points throughout this paper I have admitted that much that we do is pragmatic—to use a popular word—and that our methods work much better in practice than they sound as though they would in theory. I hope that my submissions will cause you, when evolving or applying your economic theories of local authority capital investment, to spare more than a casual thought for the problems of the day-to-day administrators.

Appendix 1   Local authority loan debt—England and Wales
(Latest published complete figures)

1 Loan debt at 31 March	1961	1965
(a) By Service	£m	£m
Housing—assisted schemes	3,650	4,650
Housing—house loans	400	700
Total housing	**4,050**	**5,350**
Education	**700**	**1,000**
Sewerage and sewage disposal	200	400
Highways	100	150
Town and Country Planning	100	150
Other rate fund services	350	700
Total rate fund excluding housing and education	**750**	**1,400**
Water	300	450
Other trading services	200	200
Total trading	**500**	**650**
Total all services	**6,000**	**8,400**

(b) By form of debt (estimated)	£m	£m
Stock	500	1,050
Mortgages and local bonds	1,350	2,250
PWLB	2,750	2,750
Temporary loans	950	1,600
Negotiable bonds	—	50
Other	450	700
Total all forms	**6,000**	**8,400**

2 Average rate of interest %	£ s d	£ s d
Year ended 31 March	4 7 2	4 17 3

3 Net debt per head of population	£	£
Housing	88	113
Trading	11	14
Other	31	49
Total at 31 March	**130**	**176**

4 Debt charges	£m	£m
Housing	212	307
Education	61	96
Other rate fund services	64	113
Trading	37	47
Total year ended 31 March	**374**	**563**

Appendix 2   Loan repayment

The fractional instalment, 3%, 5% and 6% sinking fund bases of loan repayment are illustrated in the following tables. They show the annual repayments of principal and interest for a £1,000 loan over 10 years, with interest charged on the outstanding balance at 6%.

The 6% sinking fund, where the assumed rate of accumulation of the fund is the same as the interest on the outstanding balance, is a true annuity.

Year	Equal annual instalment			3% sinking fund		
	Principal	Interest	Total	Principal	Interest	Total
	£	£	£	£	£	£
1	100	60	160	87	60	147
2	100	54	154	90	55	145
3	100	48	148	92	49	141
4	100	42	142	96	44	140
5	100	36	136	98	38	136
6	100	30	130	101	32	133
7	100	24	124	104	26	130
8	100	18	118	107	20	127
9	100	12	112	110	14	124
10	100	6	106	115	7	122
	1,000	**330**	**1,330**	**1,000**	**345**	**1,345**

	5% sinking fund			6% sinking fund		
	£	£	£	£	£	£
1	80	60	140	76	60	136
2	83	55	138	80	56	136
3	88	50	138	85	51	136
4	92	45	137	90	46	136
5	96	40	136	96	40	136
6	102	34	136	102	34	136
7	106	28	134	108	28	136
8	112	21	133	114	22	136
9	118	14	132	121	15	136
10	123	7	130	128	8	136
	1,000	**354**	**1,354**	**1,000**	**360**	**1,360**

Summary—showing the differences between the methods

	Equal annual instalment	3% sinking fund	5% sinking fund	6% sinking fund
	£	£	£	£
Interest cost	330	345	354	360
Principal—difference between 1st and 10th years	Nil	+28	+43	+52
Principal and interest —difference between 1st and 10th years	−54	−25	−10	Nil

5

R L Meek

Public authority pricing

This paper is concerned with some of the general principles which guide or ought to guide public authorities when they are putting prices on the goods and services they produce. It concentrates on two questions which seem to me to be quite crucial, and which are very much matters of controversy at the moment: (*a*) How far should profit be a constituent element of the price fixed? and (*b*) In so far as the price is fixed so as to reflect 'cost', should this be average cost or marginal cost?

I would emphasize, however, that there are besides these many other important public authority pricing problems with which I shall not be dealing—most notably, the problem of which publicly produced goods and services should in fact have prices put on them at all. Some, like defence and justice, could not in fact be priced; but there are others, like medical services, roads and education, which could be but in our society on the whole are not: they are paid for through the budget instead. The question of whether these goods and services should be priced or not, I simply leave on one side. Given that it has been decided to sell certain publicly produced goods and services at defined prices, what is the answer to our two basic questions?

Economists are accustomed nowadays to divide enterprises into two kinds—the 'price-takers', usually small firms in a large competitive industry, which have to take the price of the product as given by the market and adjust their output to it; and the 'price-makers', who have a greater or lesser degree of power to set their own prices, and do in fact up to a point exercise this power. All monopolists, whether private or public, are of course 'price-makers'. What distinguishes the public from the
110

private monopolist is the motive lying behind this price-making. Even here, of course, there is some similarity; both the private and the public monopolist, for example, are concerned when formulating their price policies to reduce the uncertainty with which they are faced in long-term planning. But whereas the private monopolist's price policy is directed towards a private interest—whether the maximization of profit beloved by the textbook monopolist or something else—the public monopolist's price policy is (or at any rate ought to be) directed towards the public interest. But what is the public interest? There has recently been an important change of attitude towards this question. In order to study this change of attitude, it is useful to distinguish between two historical periods—the first running from the time of the post-war nationalization acts to 1961, and the second from 1961 to the present day.

In the period immediately following nationalization, the nationalized industries were severely discouraged, both by statute and by the policy of successive governments, from setting prices high enough to allow them to make profits. The nationalizing statutes usually contained what later came to be known as a 'break-even clause', which in effect called upon the industry concerned to earn revenues that would be not less than sufficient to allow it to break even, taking one year with another. Legally speaking, the break-even clauses did not preclude the nationalized industries from making profits. But no time period was laid down for breaking even, and no indication was given as to whether it was proper or improper for an industry to try to do more than break even; and the clauses were in fact interpreted by successive governments as prescribing a maximum rather than a minimum performance. The reasons for this interpretation were many and various. Originally, perhaps, the main reason was the traditional socialist idea that profits were inherently bad, since they were the fruit of exploitation. In later years, however, this reason tended to recede into the background, and a greater degree of influence was exerted by such factors as the political unpopularity of high prices and the necessity for controlling inflation. But whatever the reason for

111

the interpretation put on the break-even clauses, its objective manifestation was always essentially the same: considerable pressure was put on a number of nationalized industries by the government to prevent them raising their prices to a level sufficient to enable them to make profits—even in cases such as that of the coal industry, where a rise in price would have been of the very greatest benefit to the industry and would have done very little harm to society as a whole.

The deplorable effects of this policy, which soon began to reveal themselves, could and should perhaps have been fore-seen; but it was not until the Select Committee on Nationalized Industries began to investigate the problem that its full im-portance became clear to the public. As a more or less direct result of the pricing policy which had been pursued, a number of nationalized industries had experienced substantial deficits —or at any rate their deficits had been much larger than they might otherwise have been. One of the consequences of this had of course been a serious lowering of morale within the indus-tries concerned. Inadequate provision for reserves and deprecia-tion had very often been made. The terms of exchange between the public and the private sector had been unequal: the national-ized industries had sold cheap to private industry, but private industry had sold dear to the nationalized industries. And most important of all, the level of self-financing which the national-ized industries had been able to achieve was relatively low. As a very rough approximation, it could be—and was—said that whereas large firms in the private sector normally financed about 75% of their investment from their own resources, bor-rowing the remaining 25%, the proportions were almost exactly the reverse in the case of the nationalized industries. The sums which these industries had to borrow—at first largely from the capital market but later more or less exclusively from the government—were therefore enormous; and as the industries expanded the burden on the Exchequer became more and more intolerable. It was not simply that the sheer size of the funds required was so formidable (electricity investment alone con-stitutes more than 10% of total investment over the economy as a whole), but also that the necessity of finding these huge sums at inconvenient times was making the operation of the government's overall monetary policy much more difficult. Somewhat naturally, pressure began to be exerted in the Treasury and elsewhere for a greater degree of self-financing on the part of the nationalized industries—i.e., a higher level of profits.

The eventual result was the appearance in 1961 of the famous white paper on the financial and economic obligations of the nationalized industries,[1] which ushered in the second of the two historical periods distinguished above. What the white paper in effect said, to put it very briefly, was that the prices charged by the nationalized industries would thenceforth have to be sufficient to enable them to cover their costs over a period of not more than five years, and also to enable them to achieve specific target rates of surplus which were to be laid down for each industry by the Treasury.

The leading aim of the white paper was to reduce the degree of dependence of the nationalized industries upon the Exchequer. But there was also an important secondary aim, which ran parallel to the other but was not properly integrated with it—to increase the rationality of the allocation of investment funds, both within the nationalized sector and as between this sector and the private sector. This aim was much more vaguely expressed than the other, and one has to read between the lines in order to discover it, but it was very definitely present. The basic idea lying behind it can be expressed—if perhaps a little too schematically—in the form of two propositions. First, the general level of the target rates of surplus laid down for the nationalized industries by the Treasury should be arrived at by way of a comparison with the rate of profit achieved in the private sector. The underlying notion here was presumably that if a bundle of resources invested in the public sector yielded a net return which was conspicuously less than that which could be earned by the same bundle in the private sector, this was an indication that resources had been diverted to the nationalized industries from more productive uses elsewhere. Second, from

[1] Cmnd. 1337.

these target rates of surplus, as so arrived at, there should be derived the rate or rates of discount which were required as guides to the efficient level and composition of individual public investment programmes. Whether this was the general intention is perhaps debatable, but at any rate it is what the electricity supply industry, in the name of the white paper, in fact did.[1]

In the last few years these ideas have come in for a great deal of criticism from economists and others. The Select Committee on Nationalized Industries has recently been looking into a number of the problems involved and the Treasury has presented the Committee with a very interesting statement of its latest views.[2] A new white paper is expected at any time.[3]

One of the main criticisms of the basic philosophy of the 1961 white paper which many economists would wish to make is that there is really no reason why the target rates of return for the nationalized industries should be arrived at by way of a comparison with the rate of profit achieved in private industry. This is not only because of the prevalence of monopoly, and therefore presumably of monopoly profits, in the private sector: it is also because the number and nature of the goals of economic activity are so very different in the two sectors. Professor S. A. Marglin, the American expert on public investment and pricing problems, has recently said that 'private sector rates of return . . . are totally irrelevant to the formulation of public sector pricing policies'.[4] I do not think that I would myself go quite as far as this, but I would at least hope that the new white paper, when it appears, will herald a reduction in the degree of dependence of the target rates of surplus upon the rate of profit achieved in the private sector. The latter is only *one* of the pieces of evidence—and by no means always the most important one—which public price-makers should take into account when formulating their policies.

[1] See R. L. Meek, 'Investment Choice in the Electricity Supply Industry', *District Bank Review*, March 1965.

[2] H. of C. Papers, 440–VIII, 1967.

[3] See Postscript to this chapter on pp. 125—7.

[4] S. A. Marglin, *Public Investment Criteria* (Allen and Unwin, 1967), p. 92.

It is also to be hoped that after the new white paper the discount rate for use in internal investment appraisal will be laid down quite independently of the target rates of return, and that it will be completely divorced from the rate of profit achieved in the private sector. This is a point on which a number of economists, including myself, feel quite strongly, but it would take me too far from my present subject to say anything more about it here.

Thirdly, it is to be hoped that the new white paper will sanction a greater degree of flexibility in the target rates of return set for individual industries, so far as both the level of the return and the timing of its receipt are concerned. In particular, it seems to me that under certain circumstances it may well be in the public interest to allow a nationalized industry rather longer than the prescribed period of five years to achieve its average target rate of return.

One of the main things I have in mind here—and it is very relevant to the increases in electricity prices which have recently[1] been announced—is this. Suppose that a nationalized industry is faced with the necessity of accommodating itself to some big technological change of a capital-using character, and/or a substantial increase in demand. The high initial capital outlay called for at such a time may not begin to yield adequate returns—or indeed any returns at all—for some years. If the industry is nevertheless still obliged to earn a given target rate of return over the prescribed five-year period, it may well have no option but to increase its prices. Some degree of relaxation of the five-year time period at such times, if not of the targets themselves, is surely called for—and a much greater degree of relaxation than the government has in fact extended to the electricity industry.

In the electricity case, of course, the position has been worsened because demand has not in fact expanded at the rate anticipated when the new investment was made, largely owing to the freeze. But the fact remains that if all the industry had had to do was to 'keep out of the red', it could have done this

[1] August 1967.

with what Sir Ronald Edwards has called 'quite small tariff increases'.[1] The magnitude of the recent increases is due largely to the fact that the government has insisted that the industry should not only 'keep out of the red', but also regain the rate of return required by its current financial objectives as soon as humanly possible.

Yet it is obvious that price increases like those recently made in electricity are very undesirable indeed. They are regressive in their incidence; they make it more difficult to resist price increases in other commodities; and—what may in the long run be even worse—they are likely to affect the demand for the product so adversely that the assumptions upon which the original programme of capital outlay was based become wildly out of line with reality. In such cases, the only rational solution is surely to relax the five-year time period—i.e., to allow the industry concerned, say, seven years instead of five over which to earn its prescribed average rate of surplus.

This would of course mean that in the first year or two of the extended period the industry would have to borrow more towards its capital investment programme than would otherwise have been the case. But the extra burden on the Exchequer could to some extent be relieved by allowing the industry to go to the market for a limited sum, and perhaps by pruning its investment programme; and in any event the initial shortfall would be compensated for by larger surpluses in the later years of the period. If it turned out that these larger surpluses could not in fact be earned, the proper remedy in the long run would be to reduce investment, not to raise prices.

I want to turn now to the second of the two main questions with which this paper is concerned. How are the costs to which in the process of price-making the surplus is added (or in which the surplus is included) to be reckoned—on an average basis or on a marginal basis?

Until fairly recently, discussion of this subject was confined to the more esoteric parts of economic literature. In this country it was temporarily banished from the field of practice after a

[1] 'Financing Electricity Supply', *Lloyds Bank Review*, July 1967, p. 7.

celebrated meeting between Mr Herbert Morrison and a number of academic economists which took place soon after the end of the war—a meeting which has now passed into legend. In the last few years, however, there has been an important change: the controversy has now very definitely entered the field of practice. France led the way here, of course, with the famous 'green tariff' for electricity, but Britain has not been too slow in following. Today, a number of nationalized industries and ministries, particularly in the fields of transport and fuel and power, are ardently discussing the problem; the Central Electricity Generating Board has recently produced a very interesting and important bulk supply tariff deliberately based on marginal principles; and the Treasury is grinding out an official philosophy on the subject.

Some of the issues involved in the controversy are very complex, but the essence of the argument for marginal cost pricing can be put simply enough. Marginal cost, as the economist conceives it, is roughly the amount added to a producer's total costs if he decides to increase his output by one unit. Suppose, for example, that a producer's monthly output is at the moment running at three units, the total costs associated with this monthly output being £30. If he decided to increase his monthly output to four units, his total costs would of course increase. If they increased to, say, £36, the marginal cost—i.e., the addition to total costs associated with the production of the fourth unit—would clearly be £6. Suppose, again, that a further rise in the producer's monthly output from four to five units would cause total costs to increase from £36 to £50. The marginal cost appropriate to the new monthly output of five would then obviously be £14. The situation could then be summarized in a table such as the following:

Monthly output	Total cost	Marginal cost
3	£30	
4	£36	£6
5	£50	£14

It will be clear that marginal cost may change as the level of output changes (as it in fact does in this illustration), and that it may also diverge from average cost—i.e., total cost divided by output (as it also does in the illustration).

What do economists mean then, exactly, when they say that 'prices should be made equal to marginal cost'? This is in fact shorthand for a slightly more complex proposition—that the output produced should be such that the price per unit which consumers are prepared to pay for it is equal to the marginal cost associated with it. The basic idea here can be very simply represented on one of the little graphs of which economists are so fond. If we measure output along the horizontal axis, and price and marginal cost up the vertical axis, we can draw two curves—a 'marginal cost curve' showing the way in which marginal cost behaves as output increases, and a 'demand curve' showing the way in which the price per unit of output which consumers are prepared to pay behaves as output increases. If we adopt the assumptions which economists usually make about this behaviour, the curves come out as in the diagram below:

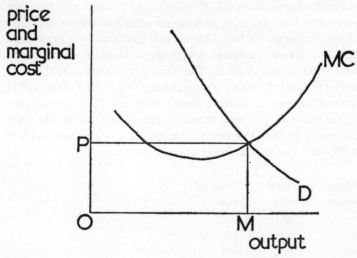

The proposition, to put it in a slightly different way, is that you should go on increasing your monthly output so long as the price which consumers are prepared to pay for an extra unit is greater than the additional cost you incur in producing that extra unit. In the case illustrated in the diagram, your monthly output should obviously be OM units and your price OP per unit.

Why, exactly, should you 'make price equal to marginal cost' in this sense? The basic reason, reduced to the simplest possible terms, can be stated as follows. Suppose that your monthly output at the moment is at such a level that consumers are prepared to pay ten shillings per unit for it, while the marginal cost associated with this output is only five shillings. The fact that marginal cost is five shillings means, essentially, that the bundle of resources required to produce the last unit of your present monthly output has cost you five shillings to attract over to your industry from some other industry or industries. This bundle, we may take it, was just worth employing in that other industry or industries before you managed to lure it over to yours, and it can therefore fairly safely be assumed to have been previously producing a monthly output which consumers valued at something like five shillings. Thus the effect of the transfer of the bundle of resources to your industry must have been that consumers lost output which they valued at five shillings in the other industry or industries, and gained output which they valued at ten shillings in your industry. The transfer, therefore, can be taken to have resulted in a net gain to the community. Presumably, therefore, one ought in the interests of the community to transfer another bundle of resources to your industry from other industries, and to go on transferring more bundles so long as the gain to the community from the transfer outweighs the loss—in other words, so long as your output remains such that the price which consumers are prepared to pay for an extra unit is greater than the additional cost you incur in producing that extra unit. And a moment's thought will show that the reverse argument also holds: if your output is such that price is less than marginal cost, the interests of the community require that your output be reduced. So the triumphant conclusion emerges that 'price should be made equal to marginal cost', in the sense indicated above, everywhere in the economy. If this is done, the community will not be able to make any net gain through any further shift in resources, and you will therefore have solved the famous 'scarcity problem' with which economists have been grappling ever since the 1870s.

This argument sounds convincing enough, but it is fairly obvious that its validity is dependent upon a whole number of assumptions, some of which are of rather doubtful plausibility. Marginal cost pricing is in fact rather like free will: almost the only arguments about it that you can think of are arguments against it! The objections to marginal cost pricing put forward in the economic literature are many and various, and I shall have time here to deal—very briefly and simply—with only two of them. I have selected the first of them because of its great theoretical and practical importance, and the second because it is very relevant to the question of profits which I have just been discussing.

First, then, let us consider the argument that marginal cost pricing would encounter insuperable difficulties because of a discrepancy between short-period and long-period marginal cost. If you want to make the best use of your existing plant and equipment, it is said, you ought presumably to adjust your output so that price is equal to the cost of producing one more unit with this given plant and equipment. So 'marginal cost' in this context must presumably be taken to be the cost of the additional labour and raw materials required to enable a given plant to produce one more unit. But in the long run, as demand for your product increases, you must necessarily install new plant and equipment. Does it not follow, therefore, that 'marginal cost' should properly be defined so as to include the cost of the additional plant required in the long run to produce one more unit? Will it not then be the case that long-period marginal cost is different from short-period marginal cost, so that if you decide to adopt 'marginal cost pricing' you are necessarily faced with an insoluble contradiction? This seems at first sight to be a very powerful objection, but its teeth to some extent can be drawn in cases where we are able to make the assumption that the scale of the plant concerned can be continuously adapted to changes in demand. In such cases it can be proved that if you are producing the relevant output with a plant whose size is appropriately adjusted to it, short-period marginal cost will in fact be equal to long-period marginal cost, so that if one is made equal to price the other will automatically be made equal to it too. The appropriate diagram required to prove this is an extremely pretty one: it goes right across the board in exquisite sweeps, and I always get a great kick out of drawing it. (All modern economists are really frustrated pavement artists!) Today, however, I think that I should sacrifice myself in the interests of not going too far beyond my time. May I therefore ask you to take this point on trust, and allow me to move on?

The second objection about which I wish to say a word or two is that 'marginal cost pricing', at any rate as we have so far conceived it, may in some cases lead to large losses and in other cases to large profits. Suppose that you were in charge of a nationalized industry whose costs for monthly outputs of three, four and five units were as set out in the table above. Suppose, again, that the demand for your product was such that the level of output at which price was equal to marginal cost in the sense defined above was four units per month. At a price per unit of £6 (equal to marginal cost), your total monthly revenue would be £24, whereas your total monthly costs would be £36. In other words you would make a large loss, which would bring the wrath of God, and what is worse that of the Treasury and the press, down upon your defenceless head. On the other hand, if the monthly output at which price was equal to marginal cost was five units, you would clearly make a large profit, so that your consumers and employees would rush to don their warpaint. Dogmatic marginal cost pricers are inclined to say that this does not matter: you must stick to your principles, making price equal to marginal cost and dealing with any excessive losses or profits by means of adjustments through the budget. But the dogmatic opponents of marginal cost pricing then reply to the effect that this would involve an irrational redistribution of income between various groups of consumers—and so the argument goes round and round. Fortunately, one can up to a point bypass this difficulty, at any rate in cases where a single unit price does not have to be charged for all the units sold, as for example, in the case of electricity and gas. The point here is that in order to achieve an optimum allocation of resources all that is really needed is an equality between marginal cost and the price of the last unit sold (i.e., the price at which the consumer is able to adjust his purchases of the commodity). Thus if you can charge a different price for earlier units, or levy some kind of fixed charge which is independent of the number of units sold, you are home and dry, and may well get the best of both worlds. In many cases, therefore, it would seem that the aim which marginal cost pricing is basically designed to achieve can in fact be secured at the same time as the aim of covering costs and making a normal profit.

There are many other arguments and counter-arguments which have been batted back and forth in connection with this issue. But most of them seem to me to be more or less irrelevant to the really important point which has to be borne in mind here—a point which is so simple that it is often overlooked. Marginal cost pricing is not an end in itself, but a means to the particular end of getting the most out of a given set of resources. And getting the most out of a given set of resources is only one of the ends to the attainment of which a public authority's pricing policy ought properly to be directed. This is a point which it sometimes seems hard for economists to grasp. When they are thinking about pricing, economists are perhaps too apt to think of the allocation problem as *the* problem, and therefore of the solution of this problem as being always and necessarily *the* main objective of public pricing policy. The other possible objectives are all too often labelled 'political', or 'social', or 'non-economic', or in some other way relegated to the status of lesser breeds without the law.[1] This seems to

[1] Cf. S. A. Marglin, *op. cit.*, pp. 37–8.

me to be quite a mistaken attitude. Economists often approach the problem of public authority pricing by saying in effect: 'The main economic objective of public authority pricing policy is the optimum allocation of resources, so that—subject of course to a number of qualifications—price ought to be made equal to marginal cost.' What they *should* start by saying, I would suggest, is something like this: 'Public authority pricing policy may have a number of different and possibly conflicting economic objectives. To one of these, efficiency in the allocation of resources, marginal cost pricing may under some circumstances be appropriate; to others, some rather different pricing policy may be appropriate; and our main job is to try to steer a rational path through this conflict.'

Nevertheless, as I have already noted, marginal cost pricing is in fact making quite considerable headway in Britain today. This does not necessarily mean that public authorities have been seduced by economists into believing that the efficient allocation of resources is the only objective at which public authority pricing ought to aim. The point is that some of the other objectives in which public authorities are interested have been found to require marginal cost pricing, or at any rate something very like it, as a condition of their fufilment. For example, one of the aims of the Central Electricity Generating Board—and a very proper one—is to prevent its virtual monopoly of electricity supply from being too seriously encroached upon. The achievement of this aim, it was recently found, was being prejudiced by the fact that the price charged to area boards for the use of the system's peaking capacity was greater than the relevant marginal cost, so that area boards were being encouraged to install their own gas turbines in order to help meet the peak demand. Thus 'marginal cost pricing' of peaking capacity became more or less a necessity, and has in fact been incorporated in the Generating Board's new bulk supply tariff. In addition, of course, there are cases in which marginal cost pricing, although not strictly speaking necessitated by the objectives of the industry, is at least consistent with these objectives. For example, the achievement of a prescribed level of self-financing may be possible either through average cost pricing or through marginal cost pricing. Under these circumstances, you might as well do it by marginal cost pricing. It will keep the economists quiet, and even if it does no good it will probably not do much harm.

But there must also be many cases in which marginal cost pricing would be inconsistent with the achievement of some of the leading objectives of the industry. The price policy which will most conduce to the redistribution of income, the encouragement of infant industries, a healthy balance of payments position, and rapid technological progress, will only by accident be that which most conduces to the optimum allocation of resources. The Russians, for example, in order to stimulate technological progress in the earlier days of industrialization, deliberately set the prices of capital goods far below their marginal cost. If they had instead taken the view that the basic economic problem was the efficient allocation of a given set of resources, and that all prices should therefore be made equal to marginal cost, where would they have got—and who, incidentally, would probably be ruling Britain today? Marginal cost pricing, it is evident, has potential dangers as well as benefits—and not only in the economic field.

The moral of all this is I think fairly clear. In many cases, it is true, a move towards marginal cost pricing would definitely be desirable—in a sufficient number of cases, I suspect, to make the Treasury's present inclination towards a kind of general marginal cost pricing philosophy quite justifiable. But in moving very cautiously in this direction, and in ringing its new philosophy around with exceptions and qualifications, the Treasury's instinct is perfectly correct. There is not, and at any rate in our kind of society can never be, any Golden Rule for pricing in the public sector. This does not mean that the economist must leave the field to the politician, but it does mean that he must look at his task in rather a new light. His job must be to indicate the kinds of pricing policy which are necessary to satisfy different objectives; to delineate the extent to which these objectives are or may be in conflict with one another; and to isolate the points at which trade-offs have to be decided upon. There is certainly enough here to keep us all going for some time yet.

Postscript

The new white paper on the economic and financial objectives of the nationalized industries[1] in fact appeared in November 1967, some two months after the above article was written. It is an extremely important and interesting document. In this Postscript, I examine briefly some of the ways in which it meets—or does not meet—the criticisms of the earlier policy made in my article.

My first criticism was that there was really no reason why the target rates of return for the nationalized industries should be arrived at by way of a comparison with the rate of profit achieved in private industry. The Government has gone much further to meet this kind of criticism than most of us had dared to hope. The target rates of return, it would appear, are henceforth to be more or less completely divorced from the rate of profit achieved in the private sector. The basic idea here is that first priority should be given to sound investment policy and pricing policy, and that the target rates of surplus should reflect these policies rather than vice versa. This idea of the target rate of surplus as a *determined* factor, rather than a *determining* one, is indeed novel and refreshing, and if it is actually adhered to in practice academic critics will have little to complain of under this head.

So far as the discount rate for use in internal investment appraisal is concerned, this will henceforth be laid down quite independently of the target rates of return (as is implied in what has just been said), and the rate will be fixed at the same level (8%) for all the nationalized industries concerned. So far so good; but the Government has unfortunately not seen fit to divorce the discount rate from the rate of profit achieved in the private sector. The rate of 8%, the white paper says, 'is broadly consistent, having regard to differing circumstances in relation

[1] Cmnd 3437 (HMSO, London, 1967).

125

to tax, investment grants, etc., with the average rate of return in real terms looked for on low-risk projects in the private sector in recent years'. This statement is somewhat ambiguous, but it is at least open to the interpretation that what the Government is doing is to compare the prescribed discount rate of 8%, which presumably ought to reflect the *rate of return on capital at the margin*, with the *average rate of profit* in the private sector. If this is so, then like is simply not being compared with like. If a comparison with the private sector is to be made at all (which is itself debatable), it should surely be with the rate of discount normally used for investment appraisal in the private sector—which is probably appreciably less than 8%.

The comments in my article on the desirability of sanctioning a greater degree of flexibility in the target rates of return set for individual industries were made, of course, on the assumption that the target rates would continue as before to be determining rather than determined. It is not easy to deduce from the text of the white paper what the Government would do under the new regime if a case similar to that of electricity (as described in the article) occurred again. One may perhaps take comfort from the fact that the length of the period of time over which the prescribed rate of return must be earned is stated in a rather less categorical way than in the 1961 white paper, and also from the statement that 'it follows from the fact that targets should reflect sound investment and pricing policy and not vice versa that if there are significant changes in the circumstances of an industry the Government would be ready to review its target within the period for which it has been set and revise it upwards or downwards'. On the other hand there are some rather sinister remarks in another part of the white paper about the danger of incurring revenue deficits if long-run marginal cost pricing is strictly adhered to at times of rapid technical innovation, and one should not too hastily assume that if cases similar to that of electricity recur the measures adopted to deal with them will be substantially different.

Finally, it should be noted that the Treasury's new marginal cost pricing philosophy, to which reference is made in the second part of my article, is spelt out in a very interesting and sophisticated way in the new white paper, although I am not very confident that either of the two objections to marginal cost pricing which I singled out for mention in my article have been adequately dealt with.

6

M H Peston

Reflections on public authority investment

One of the most remarkable developments in public policy of the past six years or so has been the growth of interest by officials, politicians, and the boards of nationalized industries in efficient investment decision-making. Several forces have been at work here. There has been Treasury concern with the financing of nationalized industries, which allegedly imposed a burden on the tax system. *The Financial and Economic Obligations of the Nationalized Industries* (Cmnd 1337) set out the new policy of setting targets for the nationalized industries, the result of which has been to raise significantly the extent to which their investment is self-financing. At the same time these targets have been seen as a device for raising managerial efficiency within the industries; aiming at, and *a fortiori* achieving, precise objectives being supposedly a method of raising executive morale and performance. (Let me emphasize that these two things are not the same. Changes that improve the morale of management used to private enterprise are not necessarily going to improve their performance judged from the national economic standpoint.) A second force not wholly independent of the first has been the activities of economists working for government, notably in the economic section of the Treasury. Academic economists have long (really long—a matter of decades rather than years) taken for granted that inter-temporal decision-making involves discounting future revenues and costs. It may be difficult for them to appreciate, therefore, the triumph represented by the positive acceptance on the part of the Treasury of discounted cash flow and all that. This acceptance was partially the logical consequence of target policy, but more significant has been the pressure exerted by members of the economic section, notably, of course, Ralph Turvey. All the usual negative backward-looking arguments have had to be met: 'these things are all right in principle but they are too difficult in practice'; 'the real world is too complicated for these academic considerations'; 'you cannot expect Treasury officials to understand that'; 'you cannot expect officials in the departments to understand that'; 'you cannot expect people in the nationalized industries to understand that'. I can remember even three years ago when I left the economic section there were plenty of people in the Treasury, let alone the departments, who neither understood nor wanted to know about efficient investment decision-making. It is most pleasurable to note, therefore, that all the official evidence to the current enquiry by the Select Committee on Nationalized Industries Sub-Committee A on Ministerial Control of the Nationalized industries accepts dcf and all that goes with it. The Treasury evidence, in particular, is absolutely clear cut, '. . . [we] recommend that the nationalized industries should use discounted cash flow techniques for appraising new investments, and Appendix A to this paper sets out in some detail the procedures they are expected to follow'.

Who would have thought that a mere ten years after the justly famous sixth report of the Estimates Committee on Treasury Control (HC 254–1, 1957–8) in which in presenting their evidence the Treasury adopted about as extreme a conservative and backward-looking approach to public sector decision-making as they possibly could, they would ever put out a paper containing anything as technical as Appendix A (and incidentally show in oral evidence that they understood it)?

Let me add that there are grounds for increased optimism in all of this. At the Treasury Centre for Administrative Studies I have taught dcf to assistant principals and principals and although their academic background continues to be more on the arts than on the science and social science sides, they are able to grasp both the ideas and the techniques with ease. Since hidden among these people are the permanent secretaries and under-secretaries of the 1990s, we can expect little danger of a return to economic barbarism in this century. (I have nothing to say about the barbarity of current macro-economic policy both as it occurs and as it is explained and justified.) As you will see, I intend to argue that the acceptance of dcf by the social service and military departments is the next important step forward. But although error still persists in those places, their assistant principals and principals are also being offered the best economic education, and will eventually put what they have learned into practice.

The third force I want to mention is cost-benefit analysis. The most important characteristic of this is the need to formulate a problem and specify a model precisely. (I do not of course use the word 'precisely' as identical to 'quantitatively'.) Such precision involves the consideration of costs and benefits as they occur at different points of time, and leads immediately to questions of whether they can be added atemporally, and what are the advantages of postponing certain costs or bringing certain benefits forward. These questions would occur to the untutored mind once confronted with the need for a cost-benefit approach to a problem; they receive even greater emphasis once the cost-benefit experts themselves are brought in. Cost-benefit analysis itself is fairly widely accepted in Whitehall, but perhaps less forthrightly than dcf. Note the word 'may' in the following Treasury statement (also on nationalized industries).

Where however there are grounds for thinking that social costs and benefits do diverge markedly from those associated with alternatives (e.g. congestion costs in transport undertakings) the Government may wish to take this into account when assessing the investment. Cost-benefit studies may be necessary in appraising some large investments and in comparing investments in broad sectors of the economy when comparison cannot be made in financial terms because different parts of the sector are not comparable.

(I presume the use of 'may' is to prevent arguments in terms of social considerations being employed as an alibi or justification for inefficiency. My own view is that cost-benefit analysis none the less is a force for rationality and efficiency, especially

130

since it carries the cachet of acceptability in Washington (and above all in the Pentagon). It has helped to make officials consider whether problems are being approached in the right way, and, in particular, has helped the introduction of modern methods of investment appraisal.)

My former colleague Professor Whitin has recently quoted an anonymous economist working for a large government agency in the US as follows:

The fundamental principles of economics are typically ignored and sometimes even explicitly denied in [my agency] papers . . . Perhaps the worst abuse is the failure to accept the validity of marginal or 'incremental' cost analysis . . . Another serious abuse is treating dollars received or spent at different points of time as being identical, i.e. failing to 'discount' costs and revenues. At a 3% discount rate a dollar, thirty years from today, is worth only 41 cents, yet staff papers add these dollars as though they were equal. Costs calculated . . . and presented to congressional committees are sometimes off by a factor of two because of the failure to discount. A third fundamental principle that is sometimes ignored is that it is unwise to have an identical material priced at two different prices at the same time.[1]

I have seen all these fallacies perpetrated in Whitehall, but would argue that at least in the nationalized industry sector, while the position is far from perfection, we have progressed well beyond that point. Incidentally, I would add that this confirms what I have long suspected, that there is no reason to assume that US public sector decision-making is currently any more efficient or modern than our own.

Turning for a while to slightly more technical matters, the chief characteristic of an investment decision is that the relevant costs and benefits occur over time rather than at the same point of time. The question arises, therefore, of how these events occurring at different points of time are to be compared. The economist's contribution has been to point out that it cannot be taken for granted that the units in which these costs and benefits are expressed are commensurable over time. He has shown what assumptions have to be made to justify such commensurability

---

[1] 'The Role of Economics in Management Science', in Martin Shubik (ed.), *Essays in Mathematical Economics* (Princeton Univ. Press, 1967).

(e.g. to add £ in 1967 to £ in 1968, etc.), and asked the decision-maker whether he accepts these assumptions. If not, commensurability requires the determination of a rate of exchange between £s now and £s a year hence. Once the question of commensurability arises and it is accepted that it cannot be taken for granted that there is not simple additivity between £s now and £s later, just as there is not simple additivity between £s now and $s now (let alone the forward market problem of £s now and $s later), one is led inevitably to discounted cash flow and all that goes with it. What is not appreciated quite as quickly, and that is partly our trouble at the moment, is that if £s now and £s later are not immediately commensurable, costs and benefits expressed in any other units present precisely the same problem. Military effectiveness over time, educational values over time, lives saved and diseases cured over time, all have this difficulty of incommensurability, and discounting must come in. (Let me emphasize I am not discussing at this point the problem of comparability between defence, education and health benefits, although I wish to say that I do not regard this problem as quite as intractable as is sometimes made out.) In the military field we may ask whether the improved performance of an aeroplane planned to be in service in x years' time more than offsets the strategic advantage of having it available in $x - 1$ years' time, or with given performance but a fixed budget whether n aeroplanes in x years' time are worth more or less than $n - m$ aeroplanes in $x - 1$ years' time. Similarly, in education there may be advantages in terms of numbers of pupils involved in the first year in raising the school leaving age in 1970–1, but if educational resources are particularly scarce for the next three years the value of using them in other parts of education may more than offset the extra cost of raising the school leaving age in 1972 or even 1975. In health the classical choice between prevention and cure is clearly a dynamic one and requires no further comment. I am not saying that in the various departments many people are thinking this way, although I believe a few are beginning to do so. The more important consideration at the moment is that these problems

132

exist, and are therefore solved implicitly if not efficiently, whether or not any officials or their advisers are aware of them.

The fact that there is no need for there to be a stream of revenue for the discounting formulation of a problem to be the correct one is not easy to get over to non-economists. It is important, however, to emphasize its usefulness even when we are not yet able to undertake a full cost-benefit analysis and measure various social benefits. One obvious example is that when discount rates rise we must consider throughout the public sector whether we wish to switch to less capital-intensive techniques with relatively earlier benefits and relatively later cost. In addition, as we consider changes in the relative prices of capital and labour over time we must ask whether it is advantageous to change the capital–labour ratios in such activities as teaching, defence, medicine, and housing rather than continuing to allow them to be determined on what are alleged to be grounds of technical efficiency.

The acceptance of the need to discount is only a first step on the path towards the optimum investment decision even when it is recognized that the discounting procedure must be applied quite broadly across all public authorities (i.e. the nationalized industries, social services, defence, management of the civil service). The second step is the determination of the correct rate of discount. The view accepted by the Treasury (again in evidence to the Select Committee on Nationalized Industries) is that the discount rate to be applied to nationalized industries' investment is the rate of return on investment in the private sector.

. . . The Government's policy is to treat the industries as commercial bodies and the underlying concept behind the control of nationalized industries by rate of return is that the most efficient distribution of goods and services can only be secured if investments are made where the return to the economy is greatest. Thus investments other than those justified by special social or wider economic reasons should not be undertaken by one industry or firm if the capital required could produce a greater return in another.

Bearing in mind that nationalized industries do not receive investment grants on the general run of their capital expenditure, 8% is broadly consistent with the pre-tax rate sought by large private firms on low risk investments when account is taken of the effects of, e.g., corporation tax, capital gains tax and investment grants.

Two questions that arise here:

(a) Does this variant of the alternative cost doctrine make sense?
(b) Is 8% a true measure of alternative cost?

I shall concentrate on the first of these, but one implication of my remarks is that much more empirical research must be undertaken before we can be entirely satisfied with current answers to the second.

The use of the marginal internal rate of return of the private sector has been criticized on a number of grounds. There is, firstly, the blanket objection of second best which casts doubt on any optimality condition derived from the model of perfect competition. Secondly, it is sometimes argued that the capital market itself is far from perfect. Thirdly, there is the view that collective time preference, even based on individualistic assumptions, differs from private time preference. Fourthly, it is perfectly possible for politicians to take a paternalistic view of social time preference. Fifthly, it can hardly be contended that any rates of return or rates of interest observed in practice can be taken as given by the Government, since all of them are influenced by existing tax policy and monetary policy.

Of these considerations, I certainly accept that pure paternalistism is a formally acceptable one, and it would be a contradiction in terms for the government to give no weight to its own views of the correct rate of exchange between present and future benefits. I would say, however, that if this is the case, it does not necessarily follow that in an economy with growing or even accelerating real income per capita the paternalist discount rate should be below the private rate of return. Secondly, if it makes sense for a government to impose its paternalistic rate in the public sector, it surely follows that steps should be taken to bring the private sector into line by appropriate tax and subsidy policies directed at investment and saving. Having said that, it is not easy to infer anything definite about government views from observation of existing policies. It is even more difficult to find evidence to support the view that overall a Labour government will discount the future at a lower rate than a Conservative one. Clearly, investment is subsidized; saving is both subsidized in some ways (tax concessions for insurance, premium bonds, savings certificates), and unduly taxed in others (i.e. the distinction between earned and unearned income). Tax policy may lower the private sector propensity to save; it certainly lowers private saving. Total saving of the whole economy may be increased because of the public sector propensity to save. At a guess, and no more, the net effect of public policy may be to increase investment and lower the private marginal rate of return.

Of the other considerations, the crucial question that arises concerns what is to be taken as given. In particular, is the form and structure of markets to be left alone and the public sector optimized relative to private sector saving and investment schedules and rates of return, or are these themselves to be moved in the direction of social time preference and optimality? As I have already remarked, what does 'taking them as given' mean given the extent of public sector activity which already exists?

Apart from this there is the problem of deciding what rate of return one is looking for in the private sector. Private individuals save at widely differing rates of interest, and it is clear that there are net additions to saving at negative real rates of interest in some years. Where the saving is through the private sector, it is not clear that it is channelled to investment in such a way, allowing for risk, that all firms have access to funds on the same terms, or that the marginal productivity of aggregate investment in any sense equals the marginal time preference of saving. Without being an expert in the monetary field, it seems to me that equilibrium in the long-run capital market is much more complicated and much less perfect (in the allocative sense) than that. (In the comparative static sense I would be more willing to believe that a reduction in time preference leading to more saving would on average lower, or not increase, the internal rate of return to private investment.)

The question of whether the opportunity cost of public sector investment is to be looked for in private sector investment or in private sector saving is an extremely serious one. It is by no means obvious that an increase of £1m in public sector investment will be met by an equivalent decrease in private sector investment. It is equally by no means obvious that the correct way to treat private sector investment is at its face value and marginal private rate of return rather than at a higher value (determined by the shadow price of capital) and a social time preference rate of return indicated by the interest paid on some form of national savings. Do not forget that the introduction of social time preference is not entirely at the expense of opportunity cost because of the revaluing of private sector investment by a shadow price of capital. (Let me add that I do believe that the Treasury may have something like a shadow price of capital in mind because a project having a non-negative present value at the assigned rate of interest is only the first test that it has to pass.)

Concerning the private rate of return, presumably this must include all the proceeds of the investment project *including* the taxes, both direct and indirect, that are levied on it. It must be remembered that the new financial targets of Cmnd 1337 are equivalent to levying indirect taxes on the goods and services produced by the nationalized industries, and these surpluses are not deducted before computing the value of public sector investment.

To summarize all of this, it seems to me that an increment of public investment can have opportunity costs of many different types depending on how the government finances it. It can be solely at the expense of private sector investment, or of private sector consumption, or of public consumption. Within private or public consumption it can be financed by poorer or richer people, by consumers or non-consumers of the product of the industry in question, by older or by younger people. I fail to see why either the shadow price of capital or the discount rate that is applied to the public sector investment should be independent of these things. In particular, the treatment of all public spending as if the alternative to it were private investment is most misleading.

Let me now turn to the problem of the inter-relationship between financial targets and the discount rate. I assume that the target is made up of depreciation, an interest charge, and a pure profit or surplus. The fact that the discount rate used for investment decision purposes and the rate of interest actually charged to the corporations by the Treasury are not the same is purely of interest to book-keepers and has no economic significance. (This is equally true, incidentally, of the interpretation of the surplus as a fund available for investment. It would be a fallacy of the highest quality to make the investment plans of the nationalized industries depend on the surplus that has been earned. Present or past profitability in this sense is not indicative either of future profitability or of future social benefits.)

Assume for the sake of simplicity that we are dealing with a single product firm with a production function relating output to input of labour and capital in the usual way. (Raw materials may be ignored or be treated as proportionate to output.) Given the wage rate and the price of capital we are able to determine the minimum cost of each level of output and the minimum cost curve. In deriving the cost curve, we also determine, of course, the inputs of labour and capital for each output level. The price of capital may be interpreted as a discounted stream expressed as an annuity per unit of time, dependent on the discount rate and shadow price of capital (or investment decision rule).

Given the demand curve we will know for each level of output total revenue, total cost, and, in particular, total labour cost. We may, therefore, infer the gross surplus which is equal to total revenue minus total labour cost. It follows that we can also infer the ratio of the gross surplus to the quantity of capital which is the form in which the financial target is expressed at the moment. Thus, for each discount rate and shadow price of capital we can determine a relationship between price and financial performance. Another way of putting this is to say that we have a single relationship constraining the discount rate (and the shadow price of capital), the price, and financial performance. This means that if we fix any two of them the third is determined. Put negatively, if policy is expressed by setting independently a financial target of $x\%$, a pricing policy of, for example, maximizing profits or putting marginal cost equal to price, and discount rate of $y\%$, there is no reason to believe that these three things will be mutually compatible. (In the appendix I analyse the problem more precisely and indicate another difficulty that arises.)

The position is more complicated, but not seriously altered in principle if we consider the multi-product case. In the multi-product situation the discount rate and the financial target constrain or determine the pricing structure.

Of course, it can be argued that the situation can be saved formally by noting that allowing the shadow price of capital to vary gives us an extra degree of freedom. There is no reason to believe, however, that the Treasury when varying the public authorities' access to funds does this for other than budgetary reasons, i.e. the variation is itself independent and is not explicitly calculated to make the other three variables in the equation compatible with each other. Secondly, the extra degree of freedom may well require a different shadow price for each public authority. Thirdly, the extra degree of freedom may well require a shadow price less than unity.

If this argument is accepted, an alternative to the present approach to the financial performance of the nationalized industries would be to give them a pricing instruction. This might be to put price equal to marginal cost, or to maximize profits, or something in between. Indeed, profit maximization subject to the constraint of allowing for social costs and benefits appears to be what the present policy of commercial operations amounts to and from which the targets are derived. (I would be more confident of this if the Treasury did not also appear to be advocates of long-run marginal cost pricing.)

138

Presumably, the difficulty with a price rather than a financial objectives specification lies on the management and control side. It is easier to determine whether or not the industry has earned $x\%$ than whether it has maximized its profits, but the feasibility of $x\%$ must surely be arrived at by the kind of consideration of cost and demand curves which would also help to determine whether or not profits were maximized or nearly so. (In saying this, I am not, of course, arguing that profit maximization is the correct objective for the nationalized industries from either an allocative standpoint or distribution of income standpoint.)

The final thing I want to say about targets involves the consideration of the nationalized industries in a public finance context. The earning of surpluses or the reduction of deficits is equivalent to placing indirect taxes on the products of those industries. As far as I can make out from an examination of the Family Expenditure Survey, these implied taxes are regressive, probably more so than purchase tax or the excises. If, however, financial targetry is not to be used for short-run control of the economy, these taxes are placed in a special category. Thus, at the present time the insistence that the electricity industry meets a specific target for this year and therefore must raise its prices is equivalent to an increase in taxation the effects of which are contractionary although present policy is allegedly expansionary. In so far as there is such a phenomenon as cost inflation it also adds to that. Finally, despite a desire to move social policy in the direction of greater equality and more assistance for the poor, the electricity price rise increases inequality and helps to offset recent increases in benefits and allowances. (I say nothing about the desirability of keeping fuel and power cheap as an export subsidy, but I think there is something in that too.)

By setting targets for a number of years together these particular effects can be avoided to some extent. They can also be offset by other tax charges, but that seems a rather complicated way of achieving a simple end.

In conclusion, let me stress once again the great progress that

139

has been made in the practical application of economic reasoning to public sector investment decision-making. There is much more progress yet to be made, and many more problems to be solved. (Two of great importance which I have ignored in this paper are, firstly, risk and, secondly, capital rationing.) Economists believe, and, as far as one knows, the Treasury concurs, that we must continually re-examine the principles of public policy in a critical light. It is to be hoped, therefore, that the political needs of the moment are not allowed to obscure important issues or interfere adversely with the next stage forward of financial policy towards nationalized industries.

Appendix

Assume there is a production function relating output to inputs of labour and capital in the usual way.

1. $X = f(L,K)$.

Total cost is equal to the price of labour times the quantity of labour plus the price of capital times the quantity of capital. We take the price of capital to be a discounted stream expressed as an annuity per time period. We ignore raw material cost. Alternatively, the demand curve may be interpreted as net of raw material cost per unit.

2. $C = wL + rK$.

We have the usual conditions for cost minimization.

3. $w + \lambda f_L = 0$
    $r + \lambda f_K = 0$

Define the gross surplus as equal to total revenue minus total wage cost.

4. $S = pX - wL$.

This is clearly also equal to total profit plus the total return to capital.

4.1. $S = pX - C + rK$
      $= \pi + rK$

where S is gross surplus and π equals profit.

The target or financial performance is usually expressed as a ratio of surplus to total capital. Given price, output, and the wage rate we wish to determine how S/K varies with r.

5. $$\frac{d(S/K)}{dr} = \frac{-(S - rK)\dfrac{dK}{dr}}{K^2}$$

5.1. $$\frac{d(S/K)}{dr} = \frac{-\pi\dfrac{dK}{dr}}{K^2}$$

From the usual convexity condition $\frac{dK}{dr}$ is negative.

$\therefore$ 5.2. $\frac{d(S/K)}{dr} > 0$ as long as $\pi > 0$.

i.e. the gross surplus per unit of capital will vary with the price of capital and, therefore, with the discount rate. (The division of the gross surplus into interest actually paid, depreciation, and net surplus is an arbitrary book-keeping matter, possessing no economic significance in the present context. Clearly, however, in so far as the first two items are constant or nearly so, a change in the gross surplus implies a change in the net surplus in the same direction).

Assume that capital is not an inferior factor of production, but that it is an increasing function of output. For outputs greater than that at which profit is a maximum, profit decreases as output and capital increase; therefore, financial performance worsens. In fact, at the maximum profit point, $\frac{d\pi}{dX}$ is zero while $\frac{dK}{dX}$ is positive so that financial performance is maximized at a lower output than that at which profit is maximized. If we restrict ourselves to the range beyond which S/K is maximized, S/K decreases as output increases.

Putting these two arguments together, as long as profits as ordinarily defined are positive, an increase in the discount rate will, if the same target is adhered to, increase output and reduce price. An increase in the target will reduce output and increase price. Alternatively, holding price and output constant, an increase in the target implies a higher price of capital and vice versa.

An increase in demand over time (e.g. a parallel shift of demand curves from period to period) makes every level of output more profitable and, therefore, improves the financial performance for every level of output. This means that, given the target, an increase in demand will lead to higher output. It is easy to show that price will rise, fall or stay the same depending on how capital input varies with output. In particular, even with increasing returns to scale, if the capital output ratio rises significantly with output, to achieve the same target price may have to be raised. (Note all this relates to the target as usually expressed, i.e. as S/K *not* as S/X.)

7

M P Fogarty

Incomes policy—·fishing with a line or a net?

Incomes policy is a moving target, and any general survey of it is likely soon to be out of date. I propose, therefore, to concentrate on one aspect which is of central importance for its next stage in this country. Incomes policy has a negative purpose, to keep incomes from rising so fast as to embarrass the balance of payments. It has also positive purposes, to make income more accurately reflect and encourage performance and to raise the incomes of those who are underpaid. There need be no contradiction between its positive and negative purposes. If incomes more accurately reflect and encourage performance, this will promote productivity and help the balance of payments. If the underpaid—those who are denied the chance to earn what their services are worth—are given the opportunity to do so, this too helps both productivity and the balance of payments. But there is certainly a question of priorities. Whereas the top priority hitherto has been the negative purpose of restraining the growth of incomes, priority is now shifting to the positive side.

There is also—and this will be my central point—a question of ways and means. The purposes of incomes policy, whether positive or negative, can be promoted either by overall measures, making their impact on all employers and employees, or by action in individual cases. My case is that on the negative side of incomes policy we have succeeded in bringing to bear both overall measures, such as the pay freeze of 1966–7, and more specific measures such as the Prices and Incomes Board's investigation of particular agreements; but that on the positive side we have so far used only specific measures with a rather narrow radius of action, such as the Prices and Incomes Board's encouragement to productivity bargains in the industries and occupations it has studied. On that side we have gone fishing with a line instead of a net. We have not yet seen how to make incomes policy a lever for advancing productivity and eliminating underemployment and underpayment right across the board, among the mass of employers who make up the long, backward tail of the British labour market as well as among the progressive few. A pattern of incomes policy which will do this has to be found, and I shall make some suggestions about what it might be. They will differ rather considerably from the current line of the government and the Prices and Incomes Board.

There is no dispute about the need to make incomes policy more accurately reflect and encourage productivity and help the lower paid. So far as the public is concerned, this came out very clearly from the survey of voters' attitudes to incomes policy published earlier this year by *New Society*.[1] The prime purpose of incomes policy, as voters saw it at that date, had hitherto been the overall restraint of incomes in the interests of the balance of payments and the general strength of the economy. By a majority of two to one the voters agreed that the government had been right in the circumstances of 1966 to bring in a blanket pay freeze in spite of any anomalies which this might entail; a freeze with, as Melbourne said of the Order of the Garter, 'no damned merit about it'. Now and for the future, however, voters strongly favoured using incomes policy for two more positive purposes; raising the lower paid, an aim which they tended to feel that the government was already pursuing, and relating pay to responsibility and skill, which they thought the government was tending to neglect. Two voters thought the government was giving priority to mere levelling and egalitarianism for every one who thought it gave priority to the reward for responsibility and skill, but the voters themselves favoured by a majority of five to one responsibility rather than levelling.

[1] *New Society*, 6 and 13 April 1967.

143

There is an obvious misunderstanding here. Official policy, as the Prices and Incomes Board's reports have abundantly made clear, has been very much concerned with relating pay more accurately to productive performance, and the idea that the Board or the government have been specially concerned with crude levelling or simply with raising the lower paid would be news indeed to some of the wages councils whose proposals the Board has considered. As a matter of fact official policy and public opinion are in general at one—though with important differences of accent from one group to another, for example over what is meant by the 'lower paid'—in considering that the two positive purposes of incomes policy ought to play a large part in future alongside its negative purpose of restraint.

But how are these more positive ends to be achieved, and, in particular, can we find measures which will achieve them right across the economy? On the negative side the pay freeze of 1966–7, whatever its faults, did achieve an across-the-board impact of a very impressive kind. In the second half of 1966 the rise in weekly wage rates stopped practically dead, rates and earnings per hour rose less than 1%, wage costs per unit of output in manufacturing actually fell, the salaries freeze was estimated as 97½% effective. For the national economy as a whole wage plus salary costs per unit of expenditure rose by only 0·4%, less than one-third of the rate of increase in the first half of 1966, and, translated to an annual basis, not much over half the annual rate of increase from 1960 to 1964.[1]

The very different picture on the positive side emerges in particular from the Prices and Incomes Board's report on *Productivity Bargains*.[2] The report notes, not very surprisingly, that the productivity bargains which it examines have not created any noticeable pressure on other employers in the same labour markets to raise wages. The Board give a table showing the increase of earnings for certain categories of staff affected

[1] Ministry of Labour Gazette: NEDC, Productivity, *Prices and Incomes —a General Review* (HMSO, 1967), esp. Tables 10 and 15: Graduate Appointments Register, January 1967.
[2] Cmnd 3311, 1967.

by productivity bargains in six enterprises in 1961–6. In these years the earnings of adult men in the British economy generally rose 33%. The figures for the six enterprises were:

Alcan: day working craftsmen	14%
British Oxygen: gases division wage earners	25%
Electricity supply: day and shift craftsmen	32%
Esso: Fawley: day craftsmen	34% (to 1965)
Milford Haven: day craftsmen	41%
Distribution: truck driver, Class I	61%

Only the Esso figures are above the general average, and the most striking divergence, that for Esso Distribution, is explained by a temporary failure of the productivity bargain there. An unintended amount of overtime and shift-work had continued, but by the beginning of 1967 was being eliminated. What is surprising is not that neighbouring employers have been brought under no particular pressure to raise wages by productivity bargains in these enterprises but that the Board appear to regard this state of affairs as creditable; as indeed has been confirmed later in public statements on its behalf. Am I being simply a wide-eyed innocent left over from the nineteenth century when I suggest that the purpose of the operation should have been to create competitive—or administrative—pressures capable of forcing other less progressive firms to follow suit? As an educator I shall certainly not dispute the value of good examples or of publicity for them. But as an economist I have yet to see any reason to disagree with Adam Smith's dictum that we would be ill-advised to rely merely on the benevolence of the butcher and baker to get us our dinner; or on their showing the open-mindedness, the readiness to follow a good example without being pushed, which Carter and Williams[1] found to be the mark of dynamic firms.

How then could incomes policy be managed so as to create pressures right across the board, for employers of all sizes, types, and degrees of dynamism to pursue its positive aims of making pay more effective as an incentive to productivity and

[1] C. F. Carter and B. R. Williams, *Industry and Technical Progress* (Oxford, 1957, for the British Association).

of ensuring that no one is left to stagnate at a level of earnings below his true capacity? The answer lies in levering up low pay against a hard price ceiling—for there must be an anvil as well as a hammer—and so forcing the less efficient employers to mend their ways or to release their labour and, in the last resort, go out of business; while at the same time encouraging expansion and the reabsorption of released labour both by bearing down on any tendency to raise pay in expanding employments and by reflating the economy to a high level of demand. These requirements can, as I shall show, be made mutually consistent.

Equal pay for equal work: equitable pay

I am asking in the first place for a policy of equal pay for equal work, of 'equitable payment', or of 'fair comparison'; for the 'equal reward on different jobs for equal effort and equal skill'[1] which Hilde Behrend some years ago found to be the common ideal of British managers and workers. 'Equal pay for equal work' of course raises special questions about the relation between the pay of men and women which I do not have time to go into here. 'Equitable payment' is Elliott Jaques' phrase, and I would like to make clear that my proposal differs from his in at least one important respect. He takes the whole of Britain as a single labour market, and thinks that 'equal reward on different jobs for equal effort and equal skill' could and should be achieved soon, if not immediately, throughout it. He is one of the many people, including many of those who do the practical business of negotiation, who underestimate the divisions between regional and occupational labour markets within Britain. What I propose is a drive for 'equal reward' within each distinguishable labour market, not necessarily in the country as a whole. 'Fair comparison' has become a term of art for the method of pay determination worked out for the

[1] H. Behrend, 'The Effort Bargain', *Industrial and Labour Relations Review*, July 1957. See also my own discussion in *The Just Wage* (Geoffrey Chapman, 1961), ch. II.

146

Civil Service by the Priestley Commission[1] and discussed in more detail by the Committee on Postmen's Pay,[2] and there too I must make a distinction. The essence of 'fair comparison' is to line up pay structures in the public service with those prevailing outside, whether these be good or bad. In what I am proposing there is no such datum line. Certainly I would like to see the pay for work of different effort and skill in different occupations in or out of the public service brought into line. But I am not assuming that the present relationship between work of different degrees of effort and skill in any occupation or in occupations in general is ideal or deserves to be imitated.

With these qualifications, however, what I am proposing does have analogies to the proposals of Priestley, Jaques and the advocates of equal pay for men and women, and, like them, differs sharply from the established policy of the Prices and Incomes Board. The Board's policy has been 'to try and loosen the relationship between pay within a factory or an industry and the pay thought to be paid elsewhere',[3] and to concentrate instead on the internal pay structure. I am the last to complain of giving more attention to the internal pay structure; the structures and procedures in many sectors of employment in Britain are chaotic. But this should not be done at the expense of external comparisons. More, not less, needs to be made of these to identify substantial divergences from equal pay, especially cases of underpayment. The Board's policy has also been that 'while an increase in pay can legitimately take place concurrently with an increase in output, it cannot, consistently with stability in the economy, precede an increase in output'.[4] I am arguing on the contrary that pay in low-paying occupations can and should be driven up first as a lever to force an increase in productivity, and that any risk to the stability of the economy which this may imply is likely to be amply compensated by productivity and other gains.

[1] Report of the Royal Commission on the Civil Service, 1953–5, Cmd 9613, 1955.
[2] *Committee on the Pay of Postmen* (HMSO, 1964).
[3] Prices and Incomes Board, *Second General Report*, Cmnd 3394, 1967, para. 47.　　　　[4] *Ibid.*, para. 50.

I have set out in a previous paper[1] my reasons for supporting equal pay or equitable payment at the micro-economic level; as apart, that is, from its effect on the overall level of demand and the balance of payments with which I shall deal later. They reduce to two; that equitable payment is the most effective policy, taking one case with another, for recruiting and retaining an efficient and satisfied work force, and in that sense is the pay policy most consistent with the efficiency of the individual firm; and that it is more effective than any other policy in procuring redeployment, in detaching labour from inefficient or declining employments and setting it moving towards those where it can be put to better use.

First, from the point of view of an individual employer, an equitable payment policy is likely to be more effective than any other in promoting the recruitment and retention of a satisfactory and satisfied work force. In the case of higher grade staff this is true simply and without qualification. Mobility is increasing in certain areas of skilled and qualified work, for example among younger managers, but it remains true that employees in these grades tend to follow rather steady career patterns. Entry into an occupation and moves from job to job within it tend to be carefully considered, and in so far as they are voluntary—excluding, that is, cases such as bad personal relationships, redundancy, or failure to match up to the requirements of a job—are motivated by considerations such as scope, interest and long-term prospects rather than by shopping around for immediate higher pay. Pay appears as a boundary condition which must be satisfied up to the level 'equitable' in each occupational or geographical market. A shortfall of pay below the equitable level is likely to be a disincentive to entering a job and an incentive to change it. But for this group differences in pay above the equitable level are not a strong ground for discriminating between jobs in which pay at least reaches that level.

Mobility among semi-skilled and unskilled manual workers

[1] M. P. Fogarty, 'Wage and Salary Policies for Recruitment', *British Journal of Industrial Relations*, November 1965.

and the less skilled grades of clerical workers does tend to correlate more with pay in the sense not merely of obtaining equitable pay but of shopping for the best pay bargain. Even here, however, pay is far from being the exclusive or even necessarily the most important consideration, even leaving out of account involuntary movements such as those due to unemployment or to family circumstances. Even in the case of lower skilled workers, voluntary movements tend to be related at least as much to the variety and interest of the job as to the pursuit of additional pay. In so far as pay above the 'equitable' level is important for mobility in these groups, a recruitment and retention bonus payable after a certain length of service may be more effective at less cost than a straight and permanent increase in pay. The value of extra money may lie much more in keeping employees from quitting in their first weeks or months of service, after which they tend to become established with an employer and less likely to move, as in improving their cash flow for the longer run, which they discount strongly.

Secondly, from the point of view of redeployment between employers and occupations, equitable payment is usually a much more effective way to induce managers to release labour from declining fields and recruit them in the expanding ones than any attempt which might be made to promote the emergence of wide pay differentials between expanding and contracting sectors.

If pay differentials are used to induce a substantial and rapid movement of labour from one employer to another, rather substantial margins are needed even in the case of less skilled grades. Elliott Jaques' figures on this have a good deal of support. He suggests that a differential of under 3% is likely to seem insignificant to an employee, but one of 10% may make him think of looking for another job, and if the differential reaches 15% or 20% he is very likely to move if he can. The Grigg Committee on Forces Recruiting[1] also noted 15% to 20% as the sort of differential of which an employer needs to think

[1] Report of the Advisory Committee on Recruiting, Cmnd 545, 1958, para. 44.

if he wishes to turn the tide of recruitment strongly in his favour. In practice, employers are reluctant to vary their differentials to this extent. Phelps Brown has shown that in moderately expanding or contracting industries there is no correlation between earnings and the rate of growth or contraction. Rapidly expanding industries tend to move towards the top of what in the middle range of industries would be regarded as the equitable range of payment, but not beyond it, and rapidly contracting industries tend to remain towards the bottom of the bracket, but again do not go outside it. For this behaviour by employers there are three good reasons.

The first is the tendency of wide pay differentials to bring in what the Grigg Committee called 'the Queen's bad bargains'.[1] The Committee's point, borne out by other studies, was that it is the least qualified, least stable type of employee who is most likely to be attracted by a pay increase beyond the equitable level, so that 'sweeping increases (even if they were practicable) would bring forward only a few more good men, though possibly a larger number of "Queen's bad bargains".' Jaques points out that:

If a person's payment bracket moves to more than 5% above equity he considers he is getting more than a fair deal. ... At the 10% level compulsive elements begin to enter into his attitude. He may express resistance to change in the content of his work, to the introduction of new methods, or to transfer to other jobs. Greed and avarice may be stimulated, with a resulting anti-social grasping for further relative gain regardless of the consequences for the common good. ... The reactions I have described apply equally at all ... levels. They are not confined to any particular group of people—high income, medium income or low income.[2]

The second is that, though a substantial and rapid movement of labour is likely to follow only from the opening of a wide margin, this does not mean that the opening of a wide margin will necessarily have this effect. It will do so only if employees are conscious of it. Recent research by the Oxford Institute of

[1] Report of the Advisory Committee on Recruiting, Cmnd 545, 1958, para. 96.
[2] E. Jaques, *Equitable Payment*, Heinemann, 1961, p. 133.

Statistics underlines that, thanks to sheer ignorance on the part of potential recruits even in the same labour market, even a large differential may influence recruitment only in the long term—if at all—whereas it will add to costs immediately. It is common to find spreads of 25% or more on either side of the median in the hourly rates paid by firms in the same labour market for workers with similar qualifications, with no dramatic effects on recruitment. When this is probed it often turns out that both employers and employees not only are ignorant of the real level of earnings in neighbouring plants but have only a confused idea of earnings in their own.

Thirdly, whereas employees move only slowly and stickily in response even to a differential of which they are aware, competing employers tend to move much more quickly to cancel the differential's effects. They have to consider not only their immediate situation but their long-term reputation as good employers, and are well aware that if their competitors' wages and salaries go up they are unlikely to come down. If they are to keep their standing as employers, they will have to follow their competitors up. In an industry with any degree of organization employers are also likely to be under direct pressure from their employees to keep their rates and earnings in line. Employees' pressure to this end can be highly effective, as Lerner and Marquand show in their studies of engineering earnings, even when the labour market is easy and unemployment is marked. Taking these two considerations together, employers are aware that if they try to attract additional labour by bidding up rates and creating a significant differential they are likely to start an upward spiral of competition, in the course of which the differential which they initially open out will be eaten away before it has time to affect their supply of labour substantially.

Economists and administrators, for their part, can well draw the conclusion that, if the results of trying to redistribute manpower by offering flexible differentials to employees are so unpromising, those who are interested in extracting labour from work where it is inefficiently used will do better to apply

151

pressure to the swiftly reacting employers than to the stickily reacting employees. The loss motive is a powerful one. Thanks to the stickiness of the labour market, the employer who subsidizes his inefficiency out of low wages may keep his labour and survive profitably for a very long time. If the same employer finds himself faced with the need to pay wages which match those of more efficient firms, he will quickly think again about hoarding his surplus labour. The classic case history of this was written seventy years ago by Sidney and Beatrice Webb in their account of the mechanization of cotton weaving and of the boot and shoe industry. In handloom weaving no floor was set to wages, and the industry died the slow death of a thousand wage cuts. Its workers hung on to the end in an atmosphere of misery and starvation, and the advance of mechanization was delayed. In the better organized shoe industry a high minimum was set to the earnings of workers in the hand-made section. The employers in that section consequently released their surplus employees rapidly, to the advantage and encouragement of the growing mechanized sector of the trade, and those employees who remained in the hand section continued as a prosperous craft aristocracy.

The measures required

The measures required to make equitable payment effective for both the positive and the negative purposes of incomes policy fall into three groups. I shall pass rather lightly over the first two, for it is the third which is particularly relevant here.

1. *Measures to improve the working of the labour market*
An active labour market policy, particularly in areas such as training and the location of industry and offices, to anticipate and relieve points of strain in the labour market: possibly restrictive practices tribunals, or Labour Courts one of whose functions would be to judge restrictive practices:[1] and action

[1] N. Seear, *Policies for Incomes*, Unservile State Papers, 1967.

both by the Prices and Incomes Board and by national bargaining agencies to investigate pay structures and procedures and encourage their rationalization. I made the case in *The Just Wage*[1] for drawing a much sharper distinction than has been usual hitherto between master agreements which would deal with the framework of pay procedures, the rationalization of pay and fringe benefit structures, defining the broad limits of local bargaining, with allowance for the different amount of wage drift in different sectors—and day-to-day bargaining and pay administration within the framework which the master agreements lay down. The drafting of master agreements and the supervision of those drafted at enterprise or plant levels should be the special responsibility of industry or economy-wide bargaining agencies. It would also be useful if the attention of the Prices and Incomes Board were diverted increasingly to the broader and longer-term questions of pay structure and procedure; as indeed the Board itself has tried to do within the limits of its terms of reference.

2. Measures specifically to detect under- and overpayment and to force the pace towards equitable payment

These are additional to the measures below under 3. for hardening the market and making it difficult for firms simply to pass through into prices the cost of higher wages, or to maintain out-of-line rates of pay where these already exist. Among the additional measures should be a national scheme of job evaluation to detect gross divergences from equitable pay in good time and a stronger policy on minimum wages and fringe benefits. Given a strong policy for minimum pay and fringe benefits, an effective ceiling to prices, and continuing pressure and guidance by the Prices and Incomes Board and national or industry bargaining agencies towards the rationalization of pay structures, I do not see that there is anything to be gained by encouraging collective bargaining or administrative agencies above the level of the individual enterprise actually to fix differentials above the minimum. Enterprises

[1] *Op. cit.*, ch. 13.

should expect agencies at higher levels to investigate their structure of differentials and if necessary to criticize it, but actual decisions can best be left to each enterprise itself. Proposals for job evaluation cutting across professions and industries, as apart from evaluation within a single sector, have had a poor reception in this country, and in the present circumstances of the British labour market this has been very understandable. Job evaluation measures the long-term factors underlying the normal or trend value of a job. In a labour market where wide scope is left for varying pay in the light of short-term and local market factors, inter-firm or inter-occupational job evaluation can be a poor guide to what ought actually to be paid. Under equitable payment, on the other hand—subject to what I said earlier about recognizing the reality of regional and occupational labour markets, even in the long run—actual rates of pay are likely to be closer to normal or trend values and in any case to be moving in that direction, so that job evaluation becomes a more reliable guide. It can never define the pay for a particular job with absolute precision. It can, however, forestall cases of gross mismanagement such as two in which I have been involved on the employees' side before respectively the National Incomes Commission and the Prices and Incomes Board. In each of these cases these tribunals, with a strong bias against awarding any increase at all, awarded increases of up to 25% to workers at managerial and professional level who are by no means among the lowest paid; or in other words agreed that their employers were underpaying them to this extent, and that even in a context of general restraint on incomes this needed to be put right forthwith. I have seen what looks to me a reliable estimate that a national job evaluation plan adequate to detect such crude discrepancies at an early stage could be in full working order within a year.

3. *Measures to harden the market without strangling it*
This is the heart of the matter, for here I reach the question of the anvil against which the hammer of higher pay is to strike.

One way to harden the market is of course deflation. I am not going to say that deflation is never necessary. But as a permanent or lasting means of enforcing a price ceiling the experience of the last few years in Britain surely shows that it must be ruled out. The measures taken in these years have violated Adam Smith's canon of public finance by taking far more out of the economy than was necessary for the purpose in hand. I suppose that in this year 1967 the national income will have been reduced by the measures taken since 1964 by somewhere between £1,500m and £2,000m to cure a 1964 balance of payments deficit of £800m gross and perhaps £400m underlying. I am reminded of Charles Lamb's primeval Chinamen, in his *Dissertation on Roast Pig*, whose custom was to burn down their entire house each time they wanted to roast a small pig; till at last a great sage revealed to the astonished populace that a less extravagant fire would do. We should encourage Chairman Mao to pass on that particular piece of the inscrutable wisdom of the East to Chairman Wilson. In a number of manufacturing industries deflation, as Professor Kaldor has recently pointed out with the discretion of a civil servant and the Prices and Incomes Board with more brutality and openness, has prevented the achievement of economies of scale or actually reversed economies already achieved.[1] It has sharply reduced the incentive to invest and expand. In an oligopolistic economy it has not even been particularly effective in squeezing prices, particularly in causing price reductions as apart from preventing price increases; it has been as likely to hit output as prices. It is also an indiscriminate measure falling on the just—the co-operators in incomes policy—and the unjust alike.

Do we then want detailed and continuous supervision of individual transactions, for example continuing and general price control or examination of individual pay agreements by the Prices and Incomes Board? The answer is clearly 'no', on

[1] N. Kaldor, *Causes of the Slow Rate of Economic Growth of the United Kingdom* (Cambridge, 1966); *Second General Report* of the Prices and Incomes Board, Cmnd 3394, 1967, paras. 30–6.

grounds of administrative complication, of delay, and of the fact (which came through in the *New Society* survey) that the public and the parties concerned are unlikely to stand it. An occasional *ad hoc* measure of control of particular prices or wages, or even a temporary blanket measure such as the freeze of 1966-7, may be effective and acceptable. The freeze of 1966-7, over and above its immediate impact on incomes, had a dramatic effect on industrial attitudes and relations. It was a call to order bringing all back to reality; and as such the public accepted it. As an occasional crisis measure, a rap of the chairman's hammer on the table, a general freeze might well be used again, though not too often. But a main reason why the 1966-7 freeze was acceptable was that, since it was for a few months only and as near as possible froze pay and prices where they stood, it involved only a little of the fiddling intervention which would be needed if control in a changing economy were prolonged. So far as that sort of intervention is concerned, Richard Eells' interpretation of the attitude of the public in a country like ours is right.[1] Certainly the public accepts that business must operate under some controls. But it also sees that effective business administration demands quick decisions and a reasonably free hand, and, if controls threaten to interfere with this freedom and to stop business from achieving the results for which it exists, the public's choice is likely to be to cut the controls and go for the results.

The answer will have to be an intermediate one. First, we need to focus not on individual cases of unjustified increase in prices or failure to reduce them, or of failure to progress towards equitable payment, but on the idea developed by the Equal Employment Opportunity Commission in the United States of a persistent pattern of conduct. Individual transactions can often be argued over; the quickest way to arrive at a goal may in a particular case be to start in the opposite direction. A persistent pattern, involving many transactions, is easier to judge with less risk of fiddling interference.

[2] R. Eells, *The Government of Corporations* (Free Press of Glencoe, New York, 1962).

Secondly, we need to develop in the prices and incomes field a relation between the government and employers very like that which has grown up over the location of industry. The Board of Trade does not tell firms what location they are to choose. It does bring to bear the very substantial bargaining power available to the Government, in the shape both of positive incentives and of restraints, to create a situation in which firms know that unless they take the trouble to explore locations in areas which need development, to consult with the Board and other public authorities about them, and to justify any decision they may take to locate outside priority areas—unless they make a serious effort to adapt to public policy on regional development, and give convincing grounds for any apparent departure from it—they will lose heavily in both opportunities and income. From this general approach there has grown a body of custom and practice on the relationship between employers and public authorities over location which can certainly be faulted in many details, but has on the whole produced results satisfactory to both sides.

What is now needed is to develop a relationship of this sort in the field of incomes policy. The government has at its disposal a wide range of bargaining counters for bringing pressure on employers and, through them, on unions. Government contracts can go elsewhere, including abroad. Tariffs and other forms of protection can be diminished, taxes and subsidies can be adjusted to the disadvantage of the uncooperative, investment or location incentives can be refused, hire purchase facilities can be caused to dry up, legislation on monopolies and restrictive practices can be used with greater vigour, and price controls can be imposed temporarily and *ad hoc* without running into the administrative complications inevitable where price control becomes a permanent and general policy. Bargaining on the basis of measures of this sort is a blunt weapon, capable of achieving only broad effects. But broad effects, after all, are the most that it is reasonable to expect in the incomes policy field, and at least with an armoury of this kind it is possible to hit a target with more precision than with a blanket policy of deflation. There will inevitably be some arbitrary element about this sort of bargaining, as there has been with location of industry policy. If anyone likes to draw an analogy with the methods used to enforce the French *Plan*, I will not dispute it. Denis Brogan quotes an earlier French statesman as saying that the Republic owes justice to all, but should reserve its favours for its friends. But, just as has happened with location policy, I would expect custom and practice to give rise to a sort of administrative case law which will make the outcome of bargaining relationships much more predictable in practice than it might seem in theory.

The end to aim at is a state of affairs in which employers who might be inclined to depart from either the positive or the negative requirements of incomes policy will see that the economy is booming, that opportunity is wide open for those who are in a position to push ahead, but that unless they make it their general rule to follow acceptable principles of pricing and pay determination they themselves will miss the bus. There will be no blanket deflation, hitting others as well as themselves. Their sector, and no other, will be penalized and held back while their competitors at home and abroad are racing ahead. This knowledge will also of course be available to unions and to bodies engaged in arbitration, and both may be expected to take account of it. Arbitrators in Britain have been as reluctant to take account of mere exhortations to observe incomes policy as they are ready to allow for hard facts such as the actual existence of price control or the actual risk that a tariff will be removed.

The negative side of incomes policy—are we taking too big a risk?

Would we not, however, in spite of all the bargaining power available, be taking a risk from the point of view of the balance of payments in letting pay rise ahead of productivity and in taking the brakes off inflation? The answer is clearly 'yes'. It is easier to level incomes up than down; the process of raising the lower paid is likely to go faster than that of bringing the overpaid back into line. Productivity needs time to respond to the pressure of rising pay, and in the meantime it is likely, given that only blunt instruments are available—though price control, in particular, can be sharp enough in the short run—that price ceilings will not always be held.

But there will be a number of important offsets even in the rather short run. An equitable payment policy, by relating pay to long-run factors rather than temporary and local variations in particular labour markets, is likely to reduce the frequency of local bargaining and of wage drift arising out of it. It is likely to add to its effect in this direction by stressing the rationalization of pay structures and reducing the frequency of anomalies and of bargaining on them. By discouraging the use of pay to buy a way out of temporary and local difficulties it diverts attention, as the Prices and Incomes Board has tried to do, from pay to improved methods of recruitment, training, and use of labour.

Equitable payment or equal pay for equal work is also a principle which the public approves, as Behrend and others have shown, and round which public support can be rallied for the positive side of incomes policy. A difficulty hitherto has been that the public has seen a clear principle in the pay freeze, but none on the more positive side. Equal pay is not a principle which can be applied with great precision. Following Jaques, it looks as if a policy which gets the answer right within $\pm 5\%$ is doing well, and $\pm 10\%$ may not be intolerable. But at least this principle provides an understandable and acceptable general direction of movement, and a base round which to focus support when criticizing cases of over- as well as under-payment.

Most important of all, the sort of policy I have proposed, by providing an effective tool for generally raising productivity, and by taking the brakes off the economy, offers much more hope than the policies of the last three years of closing the inflationary gap from the side of production and of keeping down costs in the process. I cannot find any evidence from international statistics that countries which have let their economies drive ahead and have raised their productivity sharply—not least, as Kaldor stresses, by securing those economies of scale which we have deliberately thrown away—have been less successful than Britain with its restrictive policies in avoiding inflation and keeping their export costs down. As a matter of fact they have often done better than Britain on the side of cost and inflation, and of course they have enjoyed the advantages of growth while we have not.

It is quite possibly true that we have inherited from earlier years a basic lack of balance between British export and import prices, so that even if in future there were no greater degree of inflation in Britain than in the rest of the world it would remain difficult to run the British economy at full pressure without developing a surplus of imports, including of course imports of public and private services. If so, that is a case for a once-for-all operation to redress the balance, such as devaluation. But as regards controlling inflation from there on, the chances of success seem at least as good with the positive policies for promoting production and the revised techniques for ensuring restraint and regard for national interests which I have suggested as under policies of the recent primarily restrictive kind. And, to put the point from the last paragraph from the British angle, on that road, if we do have inflation, we shall at least also have had growth.

8

A D Bain

Monetary policy

In this lecture I shall concentrate on some of the domestic aspects of monetary policy; in particular, I shall consider the effects of monetary policy on the level of activity in the UK. I shall be thinking of a situation in which it is necessary to restrain domestic expenditure—a condition which has existed in a number of recent years. The international repercussions of monetary policy will concern me only to the extent that they affect the domestic economy; and while I recognize that domestic and international considerations may sometimes lead to differing conclusions for monetary policy I shall not deal with this problem. This is an important omission. However, in my view there is a conflict between domestic and international considerations much less frequently than many commentators suggest. I shall begin by considering received doctrine on the scope for monetary policy. Then I shall look at the evidence relating to the financial positions of persons and companies, and the assets acquired by financial institutions, in recent years. I shall then consider the impediments in the way of a successful monetary policy and the conditions which must be satisfied for monetary policy to act as an effective restraint on private spending. Finally, I shall consider briefly a number of ways of controlling the behaviour of the financial institutions.

I The Radcliffe Committee view

The Radcliffe Committee,[1] which reported in 1959, gave the impression that the power of monetary policy to influence

[1] *Committee on the Working of the Monetary System, Report,* Cmnd 827 (HMSO, London, 1959).

activity in the economy was very limited. In principle, monetary policy could have a direct influence on activity in two ways —through changes in interest rates and through changes in the general level of liquidity—but in neither case were the effects likely to be large. Monetary measures might also influence the economy indirectly, through their effect on confidence.

In the Committee's view the interest incentive effect was usually unimportant because the rate of interest was rather low in relation to the return expected from typical industrial investment, because it was in any case mitigated by the effect of tax, and because inflation tended to reduce the real burden of interest payments. There were, of course, exceptions—namely long-lived investment, particularly in housing. However, the Committee did not see much scope for manipulating the level of activity in the short-run by changing the level of interest rates, although they held the view that the rate of interest should be allowed to adjust in the long-term to take account of long-term changes in the demand for capital.

If the interest incentive effect was weak, the liquidity effect was not expected to be much stronger. This was because persons, companies and financial institutions had all been highly liquid in the previous decade, and because even if a borrower could not obtain funds from his usual source he could usually obtain them elsewhere at no very great increase in cost. The Committee could find no evidence that credit squeezes had had any marked effect on holdings of stocks of commodities nor was there any sign that consumer spending had been forced down, although the brunt of the absolute reduction in bank advances had fallen on the 'personal and professional' categories. On the industrial side, a squeeze might have affected projects planned for the future but had had very little effect in the short term.

The Committee's broad conclusion on monetary measures in the 1950s, excluding the effect of changes in the controls on hire purchase terms, was that 'the obstructions to particular channels of finance have had no effect on the pressure of total demand but have made for much inefficiency in financial organization'[1] . . . 'the monetary instruments employed left untouched the large industrial corporations which control more than half the investment in manufacturing industry and neither their planning nor that of the public corporations appears to have responded seriously to changes in interest rates. In the more fractionally organized parts of the private sector there has been pressure here and pressure there, but nothing of great moment.'[2]

In so far as it had any significant influence on the economy, this left monetary policy to act by changing expectations—and hence to act by influencing *desired* expenditure rather than by curtailing the supply of funds so that some desired expenditure became uneconomic.

The Radcliffe Committee decided to assume that 'the economy of the United Kingdom in the 1960s will, in the relevant ways, be more like that of the 1950s than like that of any earlier period'.[3] They did so because they felt that they had no evidence on the question of whether any important proportion of companies had by 1957 reached the point of being uncomfortably illiquid, and because the financial institutions—particularly the banks had still a high degree of liquidity.

However, they expressed three principal doubts:
(*a*) whether world prosperity would continue to run at a high pitch;
(*b*) whether the demand for capital in the private sector would be strongly and consistently maintained;
(*c*) whether the private sector generally, and especially the parts most rapidly growing, could continue to be comparatively independent of financial conditions.

World prosperity has been maintained, and throughout the first half of the 1960s the private demand for capital was strong. But I shall try to demonstrate that companies have come to

---

[1] *Committee on the Working of the Monetary System, Report*, Cmnd 827 (HMSO, London, 1959), para. 469.
[2] *Ibid.*, para. 472.   [3] *Ibid.*, para. 486.

depend much more on financial conditions than in the 1950s, and that they are becoming progressively more dependent upon external sources of funds; that consumption expenditure has also been influenced by credit conditions generally, and not only by changes in the controls applied to hire purchase and other forms of consumer instalment credit; but that nevertheless until recently monetary policy was comparatively ineffective because the banks and other financial institutions were able to provide the bulk of the funds which the non-financial private sector required.

II The evidence: personal sector

Two articles which were published in the Bank of England *Quarterly Bulletin* within the last year have some bearing on these matters. The first[1] examined financial flows for the personal sector over a 15-year period, giving some emphasis to the influence of borrowing on personal consumption (especially on purchases of durable goods, and on investment in housing). The article showed that changes in purchases of durables were strongly influenced by changes in 'borrowing for consumption', a term which included not only consumer instalment debt (which the Radcliffe Committee recognized as having a powerful effect on purchases of durables), but also 'personal and professional' borrowing from banks, other than estimated borrowing for house purchases. The Radcliffe Committee were very doubtful whether consumption was affected by changes in personal and professional borrowing.

If borrowing for consumption merely stimulated a diversion of expenditure from perishable goods to durables it would not matter much. There would be no effect on aggregate expenditure; and in principle the resources released by a decline in the demand for durables would be available to increase the supply of perishables. But in fact an increase in borrowing raised total consumption expenditure: spending on durables was a

[1] 'Personal Saving and Financial Investment: 1951–65', *Quarterly Bulletin*, vol. 6, no. 3, pp. 246–56 (Bank of England, London, 1966).

substitute for saving rather than for spending on perishables. The savings ratio tended to be high when real personal disposable income was growing fast and when borrowing for consumption was low. Conversely the savings ratio was low when incomes grew slowly or borrowing was high. In the published article, there was no statistical analysis of these two determinants of the savings ratio, but their effects can in fact be distinguished.

The behaviour of consumption in recent years has shown that a combination of constraints on the availability of funds to personal borrowers and an increase in their cost have a substantial effect on consumption. Greater availability has usually been associated with lower cost, and it is not easy to distinguish between the two effects; but so long as changes do go together a distinction is unnecessary. There is also some evidence, though it has not been demonstrated conclusively by statistical analysis, that consumption is affected in the short term by changes in asset prices: capital gains in stocks and shares seem to stimulate personal consumption. In so far as fluctuations in the yields on equities and on fixed interest stocks—as opposed to changes in the availability of funds—influence consumption, it may well be in this way.

The Radcliffe Committee had no doubt that changes in interest rates and in the supply of funds affected private housebuilding. It is not difficult to find good reasons for this. The percentage of income devoted to mortgage payments for a given sum borrowed rises with the rate of interest charged; and building society conventions limit this percentage. In periods of high interest rates some potential borrowers may be deterred from going to insurance companies by the high, and often fixed, rates of interest charged; and with stock market conditions depressed a feeling that it is not a good time to sell shares may deter some potential purchasers of relatively high priced houses. Nevertheless, so long as the cost remains within the range to which we have been accustomed, changes in cost are probably less important than changes in the supply of funds.

There is a clear connection between house-building by the personal sector and total mortgage borrowing. When interest rates rise generally building society rates often tend to lag behind, and the funds which they have available to lend are less than the demands upon them; so building societies reduce the percentage of the price which they are prepared to advance and turn down potential borrowers, many of whom would not be attractive to other lenders, such as insurance companies. If at the same time the banks impose a strict interpretation on 'bridging loans'—granting them only when the purchaser of a house has a firm contract for the sale of his own—funds are withdrawn from the housing market, because fewer people own two houses. Experience in the last few years leaves no doubt that monetary policy still has a powerful effect on the housing market and on new private house-building.

III The evidence: company sector

The second article in the Bank of England *Quarterly Bulletin*[1] showed that the financial condition of companies has changed since the 1950s. Companies have come to depend much more on external sources of funds to finance their capital expenditure in recent years than in the period reviewed by the Radcliffe Committee. Taking a broad definition of capital expenditure (gross fixed investment, stock building, investment abroad, purchase of UK company securities, changes in hire purchase credit extended and the unidentified item which includes trade credit extended), internal funds (saving) contributed 85% of the funds required for companies' capital expenditure in 1952/58 but only 71% in 1959/65. Throughout the entire period, in the expansion phase of the cycle companies financed a relatively large part of their capital expenditure from borrowing or by running down (or failing to build up) liquid assets, even though in these years internal funds tended to rise rapidly because

[1] 'Company Finance: 1952–65', *Quarterly Bulletin*, vol. 7, no. 1, pp. 29–42 (Bank of England, London, 1967).

profits were large and tax payments were determined by the lower profits of earlier years.

The relative importance of borrowing and sales of liquid asset holdings in comparison with internal funds has greatly increased in successive cycles. Borrowing and changes in liquid assets financed about 19% of capital expenditure in the 1954–5 upswing, about 25% in the 1960–1, and about 29% in 1964–5. The absolute amounts involved are considerable—over £1,300m in 1964 and over £1,000m in 1965. In 1964 and 1965 together industrial and commercial companies borrowed nearly £1,200m from the banks, raised £800m through the capital market (almost record levels), £400m from other sources (including the public sector), and added remarkably little to their liquid asset holdings.

Is it a fair inference that, with magnitudes of this order, a substantial cut in bank lending to companies would have had a significant effect on companies' expenditure? I believe that it is. Of course, a withdrawal of funds from this particular source might well have been partly offset by an increase in funds obtained in other ways, or by a reduction in liquid asset holdings. In recent years it seems to me that the scope for this has been rather limited. When companies' demands have been at a peak, insurance companies and pension funds have allocated the bulk of their funds to the private sector, and most of these funds were lent in one way or other to companies. Such lending could have been increased only by net sales of public sector debt, which was not very likely because the proportion of gilt-edged securities in their portfolios had already been reduced substantially, or by lending less to persons, which would have been difficult (since the right to borrow is often a condition of the policy) and which, if it had occurred, would have cut back personal expenditure. Since holdings of liquid assets were at a level which caused considerable concern to many companies by the end of 1965, the scope for a further general reduction was also very limited.

Even if companies' capital expenditure had been cut, it could be argued that the cuts would have been concentrated on

167

the items other than fixed domestic capital formation and stock building: capital expenditure has been defined to include cash required for take-overs of other companies, overseas investment, and the unidentified item in the statistics. Certainly, by no means all of any cut in capital expenditure would have been reflected in a reduction in companies' expenditure on goods and services in the United Kingdom. It is highly likely that take-overs of other companies for cash would have been reduced. But, while the position of companies which would otherwise have expanded through take-overs would have been eased, it would have been more difficult for other companies to raise funds in the market, because a reduction in the funds paid out in take-overs would have reduced in turn the amount of funds which persons and financial institutions had available to subscribe to new issues, and would correspondingly have further limited the supply of finance. There might also have been some reduction in overseas investment, although this would probably not have been large in that much of this investment was financed from profits earned and retained overseas which were not readily available for investment in the United Kingdom. Finally, there might have been a reduction in trade credit granted to the personal sector (which is included in the unidentified item); but this would have been matched very largely by a reduction in personal expenditure on goods and services.

Thus if companies had chosen not to cut their own expenditure on goods and services in line with a reduction in the supply of funds available to them, the reduction in their 'financial' capital expenditure would have led to a cut in personal spending on goods and services and to some further curtailment of the funds available in the capital market. Moreover, any reduction in expenditure on goods and services (by companies or by persons) would have reduced companies' trading profits and consequently their internal funds.

It is also very important to notice that companies' holdings of liquid assets were built up in the years prior to booms, especially 1959 and 1963. This was associated with, and partly caused by, government attempts to lift the economy out of recessions. As a result of these attempts company income rose rapidly, while company expenditure on capital investment and tax payments lagged behind. Had such large cushions of liquid assets not been available, the level of expenditure on goods and services in the ensuing years would have been lower. This pattern of a flow of spare liquidity in years of recovery followed by an ebb in the subsequent boom years seems to be a feature of an economy in which the authorities operate a counter-cyclical fiscal policy. If governments were less intent on jerking the economy out of recessions, they would be in a better position to control the booms that follow.

I conclude that the Radcliffe Committee were right to express their doubts as to 'whether the private sector generally and especially the parts most rapidly growing can continue to be comparatively independent of financial conditions'. However, their prognosis was based on the assumption that excess liquidity would continue and they therefore seriously underestimated the possible role for monetary policy.

IV The evidence: financial intermediaries

If the Radcliffe Committee were wrong about the effects of companies requiring external finance, they were right about the continued high liquidity of financial institutions throughout the early years of the 1960s. At the end of 1957 the banks held government debt amounting to over 70% of their deposit liabilities; and, while good statistics are not generally available for the insurance companies and pension funds at this time, it is known that most of them were well stocked with gilt-edged securities and other public sector debt. In the aggregate, although they acquired a certain amount of gilt-edged securities in the first half of the 1960s they reduced, and in some cases substantially reduced, the proportion of gilt-edged securities in their portfolios.

Taking the years since 1957 as a whole the government[1] has

[1] Not including the local authorities.

not in fact been a large net borrower from the banks. There are a number of reasons for this. Firstly, tax revenue has at least kept pace with government expenditure, and a surplus has been available to meet part of the borrowing requirement of the rest of the public sector, the public corporations and the local authorities. Secondly, the course of the balance of payments and changes in overseas holdings of UK government and private short-term debt have affected the government's domestic borrowing requirements: when there is a balance of payments deficit the authorities sell foreign exchange to the private sector and use the proceeds to repay government debt. Thirdly, non-banks have taken up some debt—both marketable and non-marketable. Fourthly, for much of the period the local authorities were forced to borrow most of their requirements in the market, rather than from the government. However, at certain times—particularly when the authorities were trying to restrain private expenditure—the government did increase its borrowing from the banking sector, because at such times the public tended to run down their holdings of government debt, or did not increase them as fast as usual. Moreover, even if the government's demands were moderate, this moderation was insufficient because in 1957 the banks had held more government debt in their portfolios than they would have liked; and they were only too glad to have the opportunity of reducing the relative importance of this type of asset in their portfolios. When their liquidity began to fall to a level which they did not want to see reduced the banks were able to compress their government debt portfolios further by increasing their holdings of commercial bills; and the banking sector as a whole was also able to avoid any threatened shortage of funds by attracting deposits from abroad.

Thus until very recently the banks and other financial institutions have been able to satisfy the non-financial private sector's demands for funds. Only by the imposition of direct controls on the banks and finance houses and the gradual extension of the network of recommendations and requests have the authorities been able to make monetary control bite.

V Impediments to monetary policy

Changes in the balance of the asset portfolios of financial institutions have no effect on the flow of aggregate income, provided that borrowers who are denied credit spend less and borrowers who obtain credit spend more. This generally applies within the private sector: it makes no difference whether Smith keeps his overdraft of £1,000 and Brown is refused one, or Smith repays his and Brown is allowed an equal overdraft. But in the UK it does not apply to the government. If the private sector's (including the financial institutions') demand for government debt falls away, if lenders in the private sector prefer to lend to private sector borrowers rather than to the government, the government does not spend less: it simply prints more treasury bills or bank notes, which are then held *voluntarily* by the banks or the rest of the private sector because their asset portfolios have been augmented. The ownership of these assets—whether the bank deposits, which are the counterpart of the treasury bills, or the cash—will change as individuals turn them over. But the private sector as a whole will reduce its holdings of government debt only to the extent that the extra demand for goods and services worsens the balance of payments or the extra income generates larger tax payments. The high liquidity of the financial institutions at the beginning of the 1960s made it possible for them to satisfy the private sector's demands without attracting additional savings. Because they were able to reduce the proportion of government debt in their portfolios the banks and other financial institutions permitted the private sector to obtain funds without ensuring that other demands on resources were correspondingly reduced. There was nothing improper or reprehensible in this. Nevertheless, it was a major impediment to a successful monetary policy.

A second major impediment to monetary policy has been the growth of international short-term capital movements. These were associated with the revival of non-resident convertibility for sterling in 1958. For some years afterwards there

171

was a growing volume of funds seeking investment, stimulated in part by interest rate regulations in the USA. There were potential borrowers in many countries; and in the UK the existence of a very liquid and often relatively attractive asset in short-term loans to local authorities attracted a substantial volume of funds, much of which was placed indirectly through the Accepting Houses or Overseas Banks.

For most of the 1950s changes in overseas sterling balances were caused principally by changes in the reserves of the overseas sterling area. The sensitivity of these balances to changes in interest rates was not marked; and the bulk of the balances were invested in government debt. In so far as balances were held with banks, changes in these balances would often be matched by changes in the banks' own holdings (directly, or indirectly through the discount market) of government debt. While these conditions obtained, 'overseas' did not represent an important source of liquidity for the UK private sector.

Since 1958 this has no longer been true. So long as there has been confidence in the maintenance of existing parities for major currencies, funds have flowed between countries in response to interest rate differentials. Most of the interest-sensitive balances have not been official balances and have not been lent directly to the government; they have therefore had a significant effect on private liquidity. Hire purchase companies borrowed heavily at times from overseas residents (e.g. £150m at the end of June 1966), and a substantial part of the funds they obtained from banks also reflected overseas deposits. The same was true of local authorities, though in their case much greater sums were involved. Some of the overseas funds were lent in sterling by the overseas lender, and the remainder represents currency borrowing by UK banks (or in some cases by UK companies) which they switched into sterling themselves.

An increase in net liabilities to overseas at times of strong demand for funds in the UK has made a substantial contribution to the total funds available to the UK private sector at such times. In the absence of these funds domestic interest rates would certainly have been higher, and some potential borrowers would have gone without funds. For example if the banks had had less funds available for lending they would probably have cut down on their lending to persons and to some companies.

VI Conditions for a successful monetary policy

There are four conditions which must be satisfied if private expenditure is to be controlled successfully by monetary policy.

(1) The non-financial private sector should have relatively little spare liquidity. This means that firms' and individuals' holdings of cash or bank deposits should be adequate for their everyday needs but should not be much more; in other words, there must be little scope for an increase in the velocity of circulation. In addition the public as a whole should not want to finance expenditure by running down their holdings of government debt: for unless sales and maturities of government debt are offset by purchases by firm holders elsewhere in the private sector, the money supply will rise. In order to avoid a build-up of excess liquidity in the private sector the government must be willing to match its borrowing to what the private sector is willing to lend it, i.e. the amount of government debt outstanding must be such that the private sector is in an equilibrium situation, rather than a disequilibrium situation in which there is a general tendency to convert financial assets into goods and services. This in turn implies that the government must be prepared to raise taxes, cut its expenditure, or raise interest rates in order to encourage saving and attract loans which would otherwise have been made to the private sector. The government must also exercise restraint in pursuing counter-cyclical fiscal policies, because when a reduced government surplus is used to stimulate the economy and bring it rapidly out of a recession, a cushion of liquidity in the private sector

is created, which makes it difficult or impossible to control private expenditure during the subsequent boom.

(2) The authorities must have the ability to prevent substantial short-term switches between private sector debt in the portfolios of financial institutions (including banks). This means that the proportion of gilt-edged securities in these institutions' portfolios should be such that, while they might willingly increase their holdings if the private sector's demand for credit was weak, they would be reluctant to reduce their holdings of government debt when the private sector's demand for credit was strong. Even if these conditions prevailed some restraints would probably also be necessary to prevent sharp short-term changes in the balance of the institutions' asset portfolios. The banks and other financial institutions depend on the private sector for their funds, and at times when the demand for credit by the private sector is very high they may be prepared to reduce their holdings of government debt substantially in order to retain their customers' goodwill—even at the cost of an uncomfortable reduction in their liquidity.[1]

(3) The authorities must be willing to deny access to overseas funds to the private sector as a whole. This must apply both to the non-financial private sector and to financial institutions. In the past three years, as we have already seen, there have been instances when substantial volumes of foreign funds were switched into sterling, mainly by financial institutions but also by manufacturing industry. We should note here the somewhat anomalous position of the local authorities, which obtain a substantial proportion of their funds from overseas. If, when UK lenders withdraw their funds, the local authorities are permitted to make up the deficiency by increased borrowing overseas, this has the same effect on the economy as direct borrowing by the private sector.

[1] It is necessary to observe, however, that this is not a justification for compelling the institutions to increase or even maintain their gilt-edged portfolios in the long term.

(4) Monetary policy will not be effective in controlling the domestic economy unless the authorities are willing to *make* it effective, and are prepared, if necessary, to subordinate other aims of policy to this end. Firstly, the authorities may be inhibited in restricting access to overseas funds by their desire to bolster the gold and dollar reserves. In my opinion, the damage to monetary control outweighs any transient gain to the reserves. Secondly, the authorities may not be convinced that monetary policy is a suitable instrument for short-term demand management; they may accept the view that monetary policy can provide a background to other instruments of economic policy, but that it is not suited to a major role in the forefront of policy. I should be the first to admit that far too little is known about the relationship between borrowing and expenditure on goods and services. Yet if I am right that there is a fairly close connection between the availability of credit and private expenditure, it is just as important for short-term demand management that the volume of credit should be controlled as that the target budget surplus or deficit should be judged correctly: there are many people who are prepared to take a view on what the target budget surplus should be who would be unable or unwilling to quantify their view of how much credit should be granted to the private sector. Finally, for political reasons the authorities may not desire to carry out an effective monetary policy: they may shy away from the level of interest rates which would be needed if no additional direct restraints were to be imposed on financial institutions, and they may be unwilling or unable to introduce the legislation and create the administrative machinery which additional controls would require.

VII Techniques of control

Assuming that the authorities did want to control private expenditure through monetary policy, what techniques of control would be likely to be effective? The classic technique of open market operations is, of course, the first that comes to mind;

yet in the United Kingdom it would be unwise to rely on implementing monetary control by this means alone. At the present time the authorities act as a 'jobber of last resort' in the gilt-edged market, and the character of the gilt-edged market reflects the fact that it is known that large amounts of securities can always be sold at a price that does not differ substantially from the ruling market price. To make open market operations effective, the authorities would have to go well beyond their present practices in influencing market prices: they would have to refuse to buy gilt-edged in some instances, and indeed they might have to attempt to sell large amounts of securities at times when the public's appetite for government debt was more than satiated. I have no doubt that the authorities would ultimately find buyers at some price—but only by creating disorderly market conditions, which might damage the demand for gilt-edged securities in the longer term, and by pushing interest rates to a level which would probably have substantial and damaging international repercussions. Similarly, attempts to create a demand for government debt by very large increases in the interest rates offered on non-marketable debt, such as national savings, would probably be unacceptable politically and would have severe repercussions on other institutions such as the Building Societies, which are to some extent dependent on stable financial conditions. To see this we need only look to the United States of America at the end of last year when many Savings and Loan Associations got into difficulties during the sharp rise in interest rates.

If the objections to open market operations, unaided by any other measure, are thought to be over-riding, we are left with direct constraints on the portfolios of the financial institutions as an alternative. These could take a number of forms. At the time of writing,[1] the most recent innovation in the UK is the ceiling on bank advances, applying to individual banks and related to their advances outstanding at a base date. Ceilings were abandoned as a means of control for the Clearing and Scottish Banks only in April, and are still in force for many

[1] August 1967.

other financial institutions. This type of control may be adequate in crisis conditions. In the short term the damage to the financial system which results from inhibiting competition amongst financial institutions is probably not very great. But in the longer term a rigid freezing of the relative positions of different banks is likely to lead to great inefficiency and is certainly unacceptable to anyone who believes in a market economy. Ceilings of this sort, if they are enforceable or are strictly observed, cause great inequities. Banks which were over-lent at the base date do not suffer at all—indeed they benefit—whereas other banks which had perhaps a substantial volume of liquid assets in order to meet known future commitments suffer considerably. Moreover, ceilings could not be used regularly as a weapon of monetary policy because to do so would encourage forestalling: the banks would try to ensure that they were fully lent in order to avoid being caught in unfavourable positions. Finally, since a ceiling on bank lending is a drastic means of control, it is difficult to bring into force, and in practice ceilings are unlikely to be imposed until it is too late.

Another possibility is to control the banks by imposing variable liquidity ratios—either directly, or by topping up some fixed ratio with a variable amount of restricted deposits. A fixed liquidity ratio combined with Special Deposits has been in existence for the London Clearing and Scottish Banks for some years. At first sight this seems the obvious technique of control to develop; but in fact it is by no means easy to find an equitable basis for a liquidity ratio control, because such a basis would need to take account of differing types of business undertaken by different banks and by the other financial institutions. Within the banking sector itself different groups of banks, and individual banks within these groups, have very diverse types of business and the proportion of liquid assets in their portfolios varies enormously. It is difficult to find a good reason why all banks should conform to some simple norm. It is often argued that if all were forced to conform to some norm London's competitiveness as a financial centre

177

would be weakened. However, I do not find this argument convincing: the existence and rapid growth in recent years of the inter-bank call money market would make it possible for most banks to adjust towards a norm fairly easily, and at no very great cost, particularly if the norm made some allowance for different types of business. Moreover, controls need not affect London's entrepôt business, because the main effect on aggregate demand in the UK occurs when overseas funds are employed in this country; deposits taken from and re-lent overseas could therefore be exempt. There is also the problem of ensuring equity between banks and other financial institutions; but I believe that this could be resolved.

A third theoretical possibility would be to call for Special Deposits without imposing any minimum liquidity ratio. Its effectiveness would depend on whether the banks regarded these deposits as a substitute for public sector debt or private sector debt in their asset portfolios. It is very likely that the banks would wish to reduce their holdings of public sector debt: first, if the Special Deposits carried a low or nil rate of interest, the banks would take action to recoup the loss of earnings; secondly, if the Special Deposits were likely to be released again in due course, they would retain some of the attributes of government debt in the banks' assets portfolios; and thirdly, taking the banking sector as a whole, there is at present a substantial cushion of spare liquidity available, and unless the call for Special Deposits was very large—much larger proportionately than any that have yet been made from the Clearing Banks—the banks would use these liquid assets to make the deposits. Of course, a call for Special Deposits could be backed up by requests to the banks concerned not to reduce their holdings of government debt; but then we should have a system with base date inequities similar to those associated with an advances ceiling. There would also be very great practical difficulties in deciding how balances with other banks and call money should be treated; it would be difficult to work out any satisfactory penalty for non-observance; and if the requests were not backed by enforcement, the effect might well be perverse, because many banks might judge that an advances ceiling would follow and adjust their portfolios accordingly. In my view, Special Deposits, without a fixed liquidity ratio, would be unlikely to prove satisfactory in practice.

I do not think it is either desirable or possible to rely on any single method of control. There may be scope for the government broker to be a more reluctant buyer or more active seller of stock without disorganizing the market—thus encouraging more effectively a rise in interest rates. More rapid increases in interest rates would reduce the need for direct controls on banks and other financial institutions. Nevertheless, I do not think that we can do without such controls, and I believe that an attempt should be made to find some system of variable liquidity ratio control which takes account of the diversity of the business in which the banks and the financial institutions engage. This would be no easy task; but while Special Deposits without fixed liquidity ratios would be a move in the right direction, in my view they would prove inadequate.

Monetary policy is now potentially much more powerful than the Radcliffe Committee allowed because the private sector's dependence on credit conditions has increased. However, its potential will not be realized unless the weapons which are employed in controlling credit conditions are strengthened. This means that there must be some restraints on the rate at which financial institutions, including banks, alter the balance between private sector and public sector debt in their portfolios. It does not entail compulsion to increase their holdings of public sector debt in the long term; it does not mean that there need be interference in the relations between financial institutions and their customers; it does not mean that their role in international finance need suffer; what it does mean is that, so far as their domestic business is concerned, there must be changes in the rules of the game they play.

9

J R Sargent

Regional economic planning

There is a common Marxist heresy, much denounced recently by Maoists, which is known as economism. It consists, as I understand it, in giving an over-emphasis to what we might call the economic welfare of society at the expense of the political objectives of the class struggle. A corresponding aberration which we experience from time to time in this country is what I might label 'institutionism'. This consists in the delusion that problems are solved by the establishment of institutions. Examples of this can be found in almost any of the experiments in nationalization. Despite the fact that the problems of the industries nationalized have survived unto the second or third generation of the institutions embodying that nationalization, the delusion of institutionism persists. For example, it has cropped up recently in the idea that the problems of providing for efficient local systems of transport are to be solved by the establishment of Area Passenger Transport Authorities. It is also to be found deeply entrenched in the notion that the reform of the Civil Service is the key to a better management of the economy. It has always seemed to me that the most important reasons why we do not manage our economic affairs better is that the problems are difficult and that the best economic analysis available is not yet good enough; and that we shall be in for considerable disappointment if we hope to do much better simply by reforming the institutions of the Civil Service.

I am here concerned with another recent outbreak of institutionism, in the form of the Regional Planning apparatus which was established—with its Boards of civil servants and its Councils of appointed members—in 1964. What caused this apparatus to be conceived is clear; it was the coming together of a revived enthusiasm for planning with the continuing problem of the regional imbalance of employment opportunities. But, as in most instances of institutionism, it was much less clear what the apparatus was intended to do, except exist; and their existence is, of course, the only justification possessed by many British institutions. From the fact that the Regional Councils have been given no power and the Regional Boards little staff, it would perhaps be over-cynical to infer that they were intended to do nothing. My purpose here is to suggest what they ought to do; to attempt to define for the regional planning apparatus which now exists an appropriate sphere in which their activities can usefully be developed towards the feasible—and ultimately the optimal—solution of important problems.

It may clarify the argument if at the outset we distinguish three separable aims or ideas that are intertwined in the notion of regional economic planning. The first of these is the idea that something needs to be done about the regional imbalance of employment opportunities, both in the static sense of the persistence of above-average rates of unemployment in certain regions and in the dynamic sense of a relatively slow growth in the number of jobs available in certain regions. The second idea is that national economic planning has a regional analogue which demands for it a regional substructure. The third idea is that town and country or 'physical' planning needs to be endowed with a regional dimension and an economic framework. I shall consider the role of the Regional Planning apparatus of Councils and Boards in relation to each of these ideas.

In relation to the first of them—regional imbalances of employment opportunities—the part which the regional planning apparatus can play is at best minimal and at worst obstructive. The reason why it is minimal at best is only partly that it has not yet been possible to bring the minimum number of key characteristics of the individual regions into an analysis of the imbalance between them. The main lacunae here are figures for regional output and output per head. All that we know in sufficient industrial detail relates to 1958. The figures for 1963, which are needed not only for a more up-to-date picture but also to throw light on how it has been changing, are still awaited. Nevertheless, although the wait has been a long one, we shall in a year or two be in a position to categorize the problem of the regions more systematically, and examine, for example, the extent to which it is true (as is often assumed) that the regions with high unemployment are also economically inefficient and backward, and vice versa. My own region, the West Midlands, showed up in the 1958 Census of Production with a level of net output per employee which in nine out of twelve of its manufacturing industry groups was below the national average for the industry group; and yet unemployment there is well below average. And at least it is possible that the slow growth in the number of jobs in the North, Scotland and Wales, which they have to bear in addition to high levels of unemployment, could to some extent be explained by above-average growth of output per head.

But our current lack of knowledge about these important characteristics of the regional economies is not the main reason for my harsh judgment about the part which the regional planning apparatus can play in solving the problem of regional imbalance. The main reason is that the solution is bound to be supra-regional or inter-regional rather than intra-regional. By this I mean that it will involve, as it has always done, favouring certain regions at the expense of others. For example, the Board of Trade has operated its IDC policy with the object of steering industrial development away from low-unemployment to high-unemployment regions. Now this policy operates at the expense of the low-unemployment areas because they have a limited amount of 'footloose' industry which can be steered to new sites and because they have alternative new sites within themselves to which they have a need for it to go: namely, their overspill areas and new towns, which they do not wish to see growing as no more than dormitories for long-distance commuters. This conflict of interest means that regional planning Councils and Boards in low-unemployment areas may have to be overruled, or at any rate disregarded, as has happened in the West Midlands. The logic of a tough IDC policy as a corrective of regional imbalance is not the creation of regional planning entities: indeed it might be said that had they existed already, it might have been necessary to destroy them. What the West Midlands Economic Planning Council wants is to steer sufficient mobile industry to its over-spill areas. What the First Secretary in charge of regional policy wants is to steer it to the development areas. And there is unlikely to be enough mobile industry to satisfy both requirements. Hence, by creating a body specifically concerned with economic development within the West Midlands, the minister may have erected an obstacle to the supra-regional policy which is required. This is the sense in which the regional planning apparatus could be positively obstructive. The possibility has cropped up again in connection with the Regional Employment Premium. The West Midlands is inclined to view this as an alternative to the tough IDC policy which is making it difficult to attract sufficient industry to its new towns. This is not how the First Secretary sees it; to him it is a supplement to other measures, designed to increase the help which is given to areas of high unemployment. He must therefore resist requests from other areas for a relaxation of IDC policy, and may even come to resent them. One can well imagine the first of the First Secretaries, at any rate, banging his desk at Storey's Gate and crying in the manner of Henry II 'Who will rid me of these turbulent Councils?' There might well be some Whitehall knights found ready with the sword.

Measures for dealing with regional imbalance must be decided supra-regionally; they must also be planned inter-regionally to an increasing extent as we learn more about regional inter-relatedness. Is it correct to think that the best way to create jobs in a development area is to persuade a firm to build a factory in that area? A car-assembly plant set down in Durham would probably create more jobs in Birmingham, through the resulting demand for components, than it would in Durham for assembly-line workers. When the input of bought-in materials and services is taken into account, expansion of output in any one region implies a given pattern of secondary expansions in some or all of the other regions, including those with low unemployment. It may be that the pattern of the secondary expansions is independent of the location of the primary expansion, in which case the latter can be chosen without reckoning the secondary effects. But it may equally well not be so. Locate an industry in Wales and it may draw its components from Birmingham; locate it in Scotland and it may draw them from the Northern region. The secondary effects will be less desirable in the first case than in the second. Development area policy will need to advance, as the information permits, to a higher degree of sophistication which embraces inter-regional feedback effects, and optimizes the total pattern of new employment opportunities, though with an enhanced weight attached to the needs of the areas of high unemployment. As such an advance becomes possible it will enhance the importance of central planning for the solution of the problem of regional imbalance, and diminish the relevance of the regional planning apparatus of Councils and Boards.

It is possible, however, that they could find themselves a *raison d'être* as the agents of regional self-help. Just as in the problem of raising the living standards of underdeveloped countries, the emphasis is shifting from providing aid and financing investment to identifying and liberating forces which may make for self-sustained growth, so are there signs of change in regional policy towards a search for the fundamental springs of growth which policies should be designed to release. The Councils in particular, with their membership drawn from articulate local interests, could turn out to supply what is needed in the areas of high unemployment in the shape of active nuclei for regional initiative, harnessing private to public energy and enterprise in the solution of the regions' problems. But this is an argument for their establishment in

J R Sargent

the problem regions, and its strength does not carry over sufficiently to justify the creation of the nation-wide apparatus which we now have, especially when the Councils in the low-unemployment regions can be more of an obstacle than a help (in the way I have described) to the policies by which the central government is trying to assist the regions of high unemployment.

I turn now to the second idea which underlies the notion of regional economic planning and sees it as some kind of sub-structure or analogue of national planning. The role of the Councils and Boards in this turns on the question whether there exists a regional analogue to national planning, and this turns on what we conceive national planning to be. As far as the most recent embodiment of the concept is concerned, the National Plan, its scope and objectives have been wildly exaggerated both by those on the right who are anxious to see it discredited, and by those on the left looking desperately for something to show which looks a bit like socialism. Properly viewed, without red- or blue-tinted spectacles, the objectives of national planning have several levels. At its least exciting, national planning is an attempt to match aggregate resources with aggregate demand, subject to the restraint imposed by the balance of payments. Given a certain rate of growth of the national product, certain implications of this can be worked out such as the investment which it necessitates, the imports which it will require, and the exports which are needed to pay for them. This yields residual figures for the growth of the re-sources available for public and private consumption, to which the government must adjust the demand for them through its power to control its own expenditure and, through taxation, the expenditure of private individuals. The procedure is of course much more complex and iterative than described. But the complications would not obscure the fact that the procedure clearly has in principle a regional analogue. Why should not the same procedure be applied to ensure the matching of re-sources with demand at regional level, say in the West Mid-lands or Scotland?

The most immediate reason is that it is completely unknown for most of the regions what their imports and exports, and their balances of payments with each other and with the outside world, are. Before this rudimentary building-block of any economic plan can be placed in position, a data-collection task of the first magnitude must be undertaken. Any regional planning, of the resource/demand-matching type described above, is planning in a substantial vacuum without knowledge of inter-regional trade flows. But if this knowledge is important, the task of obtaining it must be faced. The fact that trade between regions involves no overt exchange problem does not mean that the balance of 'imports' and 'exports' between them is without effect on their economic prosperity and development, although the connection is little understood. But certainly it can be said that the ease of financial flows between regions, within the context of a national monetary system, makes the balance of payments restraint much less absolute for the individual region than for the nation as a whole. If demand in a region outruns resources, perhaps because it is investing heavily, the gap can be met by borrowing from other regions without the frictions which exist in the case of international borrowing; indeed, the investments concerned may already have provided for finance from other regions. Even if there are limits in the long run to the amount which a region can borrow from others to finance a 'deficit' in its 'balance of payments', it would certainly be extremely difficult to assign a reasonable figure to it which could provide for planning purposes the regional analogue to the national balance of payments restraint. In any case, even if it could, and quantitative inferences could then be drawn (say) about the feasible rate of growth of consumption in the region in the light of its balance of payments restraint, the power to control the growth of consumption is not in regional hands. It is in those of the central government. There would be nothing in this, therefore, apart from the figure work, which regional planning authorities could actually do.

At a higher level of intensity, national planning goes beyond the matching of aggregate demand and resources into the implications of the match for individual industries, which it indicates to them as output 'targets'. It may well be that the planning authority has no power to see that the targets are met, so that in this sense they constitute a pale kind of planning. Nevertheless, it seems to me that it can be a useful exercise because it improves the information available to industry generally about developments in the economy which might otherwise have been unforeseen and unplanned for at the micro level, provided always that the set of targets is a credible one. Could not analogous sets of indicative targets be erected for each region? This hinges upon whether it is possible to assign to each region a meaningful balance of payments restraint; and I have already cast doubt on this. If, considering the UK as a whole, borrowing abroad can be envisaged on a larger scale, then exports can be lower and home investment, consumption and government expenditure can be higher without strain on the resources available. This will imply a different industrial composition of output and different targets for individual industries. Thus the set of targets depends on the balance of payments restraint and cannot be determined until it is fixed. For a region, I have argued that it would be extremely difficult to specify a balance of payments restraint. It follows that it would be extremely difficult to specify a set of regional output targets, especially as these would require knowledge not only of the region's own balance of payments restraint, but of those of all other regions also.

Although national planning is not necessarily connected with achieving a higher rate of economic growth—it may prefer to aim at a different set of priorities within a given rate of growth —the connection has been a close one in the recent revival of the vogue for planning in the UK. It found its main expression in the 'bootstraps' theory of planning, which supposed that by presenting to industry the detailed implications of a rate of growth of national income higher than the economy had been achieving—so much of this, so much of that product required by 1970—this would be enough to make industry reach up to obtain it. It may still be argued—I think I would argue myself—that if the target growth rate for the GNP had been a more credible one—3¼% or 3½% p.a., say, instead of 4%—and had not been made even less credible by the shadow of an outsize balance of payments problem, the confidence trick might have worked. The 'bootstraps' approach to planning is not so much discredited as discontinued. Nevertheless the extent to which it is practicable is bound to be limited, in an economy as open as ours, where economic management is hard put to it to keep a satisfactory balance of payments without impinging upon the steady growth of demand. Consequently the approach to the problem of raising the rate of economic growth is now shifting towards policies meant to raise the underlying rate of growth by stimulating technical advance, improving the quality of management and the choice of investments, and remedying shortages in the supply of specific skills. But this shift towards a preference for policies rather than targets seems likely to diminish the part which the regional planning apparatus can play, since the policies involved are not ones which can or should be mounted region by region. The stimulation of technical advance, for example, often requires substantial expenditure on underwriting research, and this the regional Councils and Boards have not got. If likely shortages of particular skills can be identified in a region, it does not follow that the action to be taken to overcome them should be a matter for the planning Board and Council of that region alone. It may be appropriate to meet a shortage of recruits for higher management positions in West Midlands industry by expanding the output of the Business Schools of London and Manchester; and similarly for other types and grades of skilled personnel, whom certain institutions may specialize in turning out for national and not merely for regional needs. This returns us to the point that, as with regional imbalance so with economic growth, the problems of particular regions call for supra-regional policies.

Is there anything, then, that can justify the continued existence of the regional economic planning apparatus of Councils and Boards? I emphasize 'justify'. The apparatus both can and does find ways of making itself useful, not least by keeping Whitehall better aware of regional issues. But does this justify the cost, both of the official machine and, in real terms, of the diverted energies of leading citizens? In any case, making oneself useful does not amount to having a genuine function to perform. It seems to me that the regional apparatus is most likely to find one in the sphere of physical planning. Here, in marked contrast to the sphere of indicative economic planning, with its array of unenforceable targets, we have public authorities which possess and are required to exercise real powers over the use of land. These local planning authorities are not, of course, identical with the bodies which have been set up to do regional planning; and the resolution of this administrative problem presents formidable difficulties. Nevertheless, there is a job of physical planning being done which has genuine operational significance, in that it results in the use of land being different from what it would otherwise have been. But the job needs to be given a substantially enlarged economic dimension or frame of reference. The function of the regional economic planning apparatus should be to supply it.

What do I mean by this? Physical planning is dominated by how to provide for housing the growth of population in a manner which avoids what are held to be the excessive costs of increasing urbanization—or rather, if I may be excused the inelegance, of increasing conurbanization—and which maintains amenity in the sense of access to open space. To my mind these considerations, which have tended to be uppermost in the minds of physical planners, are only elements, although important and necessary elements, in the general problem of arriving at the most economic distribution of the growth of population over space. An economic distribution of population over space is one which takes account of the way in which human preferences express themselves in the geographical pattern of demand for space in which to produce, to live and to enjoy oneself. The most economic distribution of population over space—we cannot yet say whether it has existence or

189

uniqueness—is the one which, of all the economic distributions so defined, maximizes the excess of benefits over costs.

Let it not be thought that the enlarged economic dimension which physical planning needs can by supplied merely by more economic statistics and greater knowledge. This is obviously required, for example, to give us:

(1) a better understanding of the influences which such economic variables as income, relative income and rents exert on household size. This influence is not made easier to estimate by the fact that we have not for many years had the opportunity to observe a housing market in which demand has been satisfied;

(2) better quantification of the 'infra-structural' public investment requirements generated by specific patterns of population growth. These include: traffic generation and the costs of meeting it in different ways; primary and secondary education, and further education in so far as it is localized; water; hospitals, clinics and provision for the old; and community services of all kinds, such as libraries, baths, community centres and museums;

(3) better knowledge of the way in which the supply of people willing to work is influenced by the industrial pattern of a region or by the ease of access to it;

(4) better measures of both the benefits and the costs of urban conglomeration. The costs, especially those which attach to traffic congestion, are beginning to be brought under measurement. The benefits are less easy to determine; but their existence is attested by the fact that millions choose to congregate in expanding urban areas for work, life and leisure. We should not forget the widening of economic opportunities which is offered by urban life any more than we should forget that its benefits are likely to be less if opportunities of access to open space are diminished.

At present planning takes place, if not in the dark, then at least in the dusk, as far as these matters are concerned. But the important point is not merely that planners should have in their hands the information of the kinds mentioned above, but that they should be equipped with a means of putting it to use. This argues the need to conceptualize the problem as I have defined it above within the framework of a planning 'model'. Models are very much 'in' nowadays, and, like all fashions, they run the risk of generating a revulsion when some of the claims of their more ardent and less well-advised proponents turn out to be dupes. But what a model essentially is, is a systematic way of clarifying and assisting one's thinking about a problem which involves a number of factors interrelated with each other in a more or less quantitative way, which is largely outside the control of the planner. The point of a model which links together these factors and tries to establish the nature of the inter-relationships between them is to elucidate the choices which are open and to indicate the consequences of each. Ideally the model should make it possible to identify an optimal choice, but it might not be wise to expect that this would emerge in a recognizable form at an early stage.

I conclude with a tentative approach to the construction of such a planning model. Consider a region which at some future date (such as 1981) is expected to have a total population, P. The problem is to divide this total between, for example, three sub-regions (1, 2 and 3) in some way which is satisfactory—or, if we are ambitious, optimal. Denote the populations of the sub-regions in 1981 by P_1, P_2 and P_3. At the same date we can imagine that there will be a certain number of jobs on offer by employers in each sub-region, and these we denote by J_1, J_2 and J_3. Let us now formalize—at the risk of caricaturing—the conventional approach of the physical planner to the problem and its solution, in the following steps:

(1) P_1 (the population of Birmingham, say) must not exceed a certain size because of considerations of population density;

(2) the residual difference between P and $P_{1(\text{max})}$ is distributed to 2 and/or 3 (Dawley and Redditch, say) in some way or other;

(3) 'required' values of J_1, J_2 and J_3 are arrived at on the assumption that so many people require so many jobs, although differences may be foreseen in the age-structures of P_1, P_2 and P_3 which will cause different ratios to be applied to them to obtain the required J's;

(4) faith, hope, and charity—but the latter in the case of development areas only—are applied to the problem of getting the realized J's to approximate the required ones.

There are, of course, obvious inadequacies in this procedure of which physical planners are well aware. In the first place, there are no systematic criteria for which of the two sub-regions 2 and 3, or in what proportion each, is to receive the overspill population $(P-P_{1(\text{max})})$. It is largely a matter of bargaining with the local planning authorities entrenched there. It is assumed that the latter, with the authority in 1 co-operating to enforce $P_{1(\text{max})}$, can achieve the values of P_2 and P_3 decided upon, by controlling the rate at which planning permission is given for new housing development. This is probably true. But in working the control valves the local planning authorities are bound to thwart some individual preferences about where to live. This may be unavoidable but the real economic cost should not be forgotten.

Secondly, there are serious difficulties about realizing the 'required' J's. If 2 and 3 happen to be development areas, they have inducements to offer. But the very fact that they have to offer them highlights the presence of a real economic cost which is attached to the realization of the required J_2 and J_3; and although the optimal solution in a general reckoning of costs and benefits might well require this cost to be borne, it cannot simply ignore it. If 2 and 3 are not development areas, the problem of realizing the required J's lies in the fact that the number of geographically mobile jobs is limited and is pre-empted for development areas by the operation of the Board of Trade's policy for the issue of Industrial Development Certificates. It is also difficult to limit J_1, in the interests of realizing the required J_2 and J_3, because there are ways and means of accommodating more employees on a given area of land. Although P_1 may be limited by refusing planning permission for housing development, J_1 may continue to expand because, for example, firms in 1 may have been prudent enough in the past to have acquired more land than they then required to accommodate their labour force, or because improvement in factory layout enables them to accommodate a larger labour force on a given site (just as the *Queen Elizabeth II* can be smaller than her predecessors because of improved ship design).

But there is a third inadequacy of the procedure sketched above which is less often recognized. Even if it is possible to provide a sub-region with a number of jobs which bears a normal proportion to its population of working age, it cannot be assumed that this is *ipso facto* satisfactory. It does not follow that the population of a place will want to work there. The range and choice of the jobs available will not necessarily coincide with the skills and preferences of its population. This problem is obviously acute when it is attempted to limit the growth of a city sub-region such as Birmingham by the creation of new towns with planned populations of the order of 100,000 or less. Even if a new town of 100,000 can be somehow provided with 40,000 jobs (a ratio roughly similar to that of the working to the total population of the UK), it is doubtful whether this number can include a sufficient range of choice of jobs to avoid a substantial amount of what I might call extra-mural pursuit of employment by the new town's inhabitants. This could be avoided, of course, by siting the new town far enough away to be out of reach of other labour markets. But if this is done an economic cost is involved in so far as people are deterred from entering the labour force at all, or are prevented from entering it in the employment to

193

which their skills can make the biggest contribution or in which their satisfaction is greatest. When Redditch was chosen for development to relieve the growth of Birmingham, the choice was criticized on the grounds that the new town was too close to Birmingham to prevent excessive commuting. The implication of the criticism is that a more distant site was to be preferred because that would have thwarted the employment preferences of the population. It is quite possible that the loss of economic benefit which this would have involved would have been offset by the saving of the undoubtedly heavy economic costs of providing for the commuting. But this cannot be presumed. The point is that the attractions for the population of one place of the employment opportunities in another should somehow be written into the model which we establish to solve the problem of the most economic distribution of the population over space.

This we will suggest might be attempted in the following way. It seems reasonable to suppose that the number of those who inhabit any sub-region i who wish to work in any sub-region j might be describable by the expression:

$$kw_i \frac{P_i J_j}{d_{ij}^b}$$

where w_i stands for the proportion of the population of (P_i) which is in the working age-groups (say, 15–65), d_{ij} represents the distance between reference points in i and j, and k and b are statistically estimated regression coefficients, which reflect the influence on the population of i of the attraction exerted by the number of jobs available in j and of the repulsion exerted by the distance of travel to j. 'Gravity' models of this kind have been developed in the United States in investigating the catchment areas of cities for retail trade, and one is now being applied for this purpose by Mr Pullen of the University of Leicester for the East Midlands Regional Planning Board. Confining ourselves to three sub-regions for ease of exposition, we can express the flows between each of people seeking employment in the following matrix:

194

		Going to sub-regions	
	1	**2**	**3**
Coming from sub-regions 1	$kw_1\dfrac{P_1J_1}{d_{11}{}^b}$	$kw_1\dfrac{P_1J_2}{d_{12}{}^b}$	$kw_1\dfrac{P_1J_3}{d_{13}{}^b}$
2	$kw_2\dfrac{P_2J_1}{d_{12}{}^b}$	$kw_2\dfrac{P_2J_2}{d_{22}{}^b}$	$kw_2\dfrac{P_2J_3}{d_{23}{}^b}$
3	$kw_3\dfrac{P_3J_1}{d_{13}{}^b}$	$kw_3\dfrac{P_3J_2}{d_{23}{}^b}$	$kw_3\dfrac{P_3J_3}{d_{33}{}^b}$

We assume that travel to work within a sub-region, in the diagonal, conforms to the same law as between regions, the distance being measured by the mean distance between reference points within it.

Consider the sums of the columns. The sum of column 1 shows the total number of people who will come from their homes in all the sub-regions to seek work in sub-region 1. It is the demand for jobs (or supply of labour) in sub-region 1. We are obviously interested in the relationship between this figure and J_1 itself, the number of jobs on offer in sub-region 1. Similarly with the sums of columns 2 and 3. Given some set of values for P_1, P_2, P_3, J_1, J_2 and J_3, the model offers us a test of the satisfactoriness of the set in terms of the extent to which it involves excess or deficient demand for labour in each sub-region and in the aggregate. Now consider the sums of the rows. The sum of row 1 is the total number of people who live in sub-region 1 and are willing to take up the job opportunities which exist throughout the region. Ignoring the fact that some may even go outside the region to work, the sum of row 1, expressed as a proportion of P_1, will represent the desired activity rate of sub-region 1. Similarly with the sums of rows 2 and 3. This offers us a less exact test of the satisfactoriness of any given set of P's and J's, since it is difficult to know what to judge the desired activity rates by. But if one set of P's and J's compared with another yields a lower desired activity rate, a loss of output is implied in this which it may be possible to quantify, although the calculation must be debited with any consequential savings there may be in the costs of getting people to work.

So far we have been concerned with testing a predetermined set of P's and J's. In such a case the P's might have predetermined values settled by the conventional physical planning approach described above, and the predetermined values of the J's might express some realistic assessment of the likelihood of industrial movement based on past experience. It would be a significant step forward from here if we could actually determine a set of values of the P's and J's which would satisfy certain requirements. We might require, for example, that the supply of labour to each sub-region should be equal to the number of jobs offered, and that the activity rate of each sub-region should be maintained at its current level. In the case of sub-regions which are development areas, we would probably require that the activity rate should be raised somewhat above its current level, since the social cost of development areas is measured in the lowness of their activity rates as well as the highness of their unemployment. Imposing these requirements we have six equations:

$$kw_1\frac{P_1J_1}{d_{11}{}^b} + kw_1\frac{P_1J_2}{d_{12}{}^b} + kw_1\frac{P_1J_3}{d_{13}{}^b} = a_1w_1P_1$$

$$kw_2\frac{P_2J_1}{d_{12}{}^b} + kw_2\frac{P_2J_2}{d_{22}{}^b} + kw_2\frac{P_2J_3}{d_{23}{}^b} = a_2w_2P_2$$

$$kw_3\frac{P_3J_1}{d_{13}{}^b} + kw_3\frac{P_3J_2}{d_{23}{}^b} + kw_3\frac{P_3J_3}{d_{33}{}^b} = a_3w_3P_3$$

$$kw_1\frac{P_1J_1}{d_{11}{}^b} + kw_2\frac{P_2J_1}{d_{12}{}^b} + kw_3\frac{P_3J_1}{d_{13}{}^b} = J_1$$

$$kw_1\frac{P_1J_2}{d_{12}{}^b} + kw_2\frac{P_2J_2}{d_{22}{}^b} + kw_3\frac{P_3J_2}{d_{23}{}^b} = J_2$$

$$kw_1\frac{P_1J_3}{d_{13}{}^b} + kw_2\frac{P_2J_3}{d_{23}{}^b} + kw_3\frac{P_3J_3}{d_{33}{}^b} = J_3$$

The a's represent the 'required' activity rates for each sub-region. The left-hand sides of the first three equations are the horizontal sums of the matrix shown above, and the left-hand sides of the last three are the vertical sums. The first three equations determine the J's, the last three the P's. These refer, it will be remembered, to what is required at some future date.

There are a number of reasons why this procedure is unsatisfactory. First, there is no guarantee that the P's thus determined will add to P, the total population which the region is expected to have at the future date under consideration. If this is exogenously determined we really have a seventh equation:

$$P_1 + P_2 + P_3 = \bar{P}$$

for the variables, and there is no solution. It would be possible, however, to interpret the seventh equation as determining a migration requirement M, derived from:

$$M = \bar{P} - (P_1 + P_2 + P_3)$$

where $M > 0$ denotes a requirement for outward migration. A second objection, however, is that there is no guarantee that the solution for the P's will not violate another independent requirement, namely that there should be certain maximum population densities. Thirdly, while the solution for the J's may be of some use as a guide to what we would like in an ideal world, it may be rather a trivial exercise to calculate them when we are far short of policies which can guarantee their fulfilment.

What we might do instead would be to use the model as a means of determining the location of new centres of population by regarding d_{11}, d_{12} and d_{23} as variables to be found. Suppose that 1 is a city such as Birmingham whose expansion we wish to stop, so that P_1 becomes a pre-assigned number. At the same time suppose that we can at least prophesy J_1, the number of jobs that will be on offer in Birmingham at the future date, although we do not actually control it. J_1 then becomes a pre-assigned number. Our variables are now:

$$P_2, P_3, J_2, J_3, d_{12}, d_{13}, d_{23}$$

and can be determined from the seven equations including the requirement that the regional population as a whole should be accounted for. (This requirement is still implicit in the analysis, despite the fact that we have shifted its purpose somewhat in

197

order to handle the problem of finding new towns for a con-urbation, glossing over the fact that these together will not exhaust the geographical area of the region. But clearly it is not possible to suppose that the area outside the conurbation and the new towns can absorb or disabsorb any difference that emerges between $(P_2 + P_3)$ and $(\bar{P} - \bar{P}_1)$.) The seven equations will, of course, be more difficult to solve because of the ex-ponent which attaches to the d's, unless we are lucky enough to find that this is not significantly different from unity.

It is evident that the procedure described does not by itself determine the location of new towns which satisfy the re-quirements of equating labour supply with demand and maintaining certain activity rates. What it does is to yield a distance relationship which must be satisfied by the relative location of the new towns and the conurbation. A number of pairs of new town sites could satisfy this requirement, but it does at least provide the basis for a search which can be under-taken by a computer programme, if need be. The procedure still suffers from the disadvantage that it determines values for J_2 and J_3, the numbers of jobs required in the new towns, which might be quite unrealistic. But there may be some flexibility in P_1 such that different values can be tried for it which may result in more realistic values for J_2 and J_3. After all, the size of the conurbation cannot be regarded as an absolute; there may be consequences for the rest of the region which flow from limiting it, and these should be tested.

This flexibility implies an increase in the number of what we can treat as variables, at least within a certain range of values. It therefore implies a range of feasible solutions, and raises the problem of choosing between them. It is at this point that we can bring into play those factors which are uppermost in the minds of the physical planners, such as the disadvantages of congested areas, and the importance of access to open space. I recognized earlier that these were important and necessary elements in the general problem of arriving at the most econo-mic distribution of population. To fit them into the kind of procedure which I have outlined, they must first be brought

198

under the discipline of measurement. This is now beginning to happen with the economic costs of traffic congestion. Are there other costs of city life which are not brought home to and taken into account by the individuals who reveal, in their millions, a distinct preference for it? I suspect that they may not turn out to be substantial when the effort to identify and quantify them has been made. As far as access to open space is concerned, it should not be impossible to quantify the relative advantage of any given distribution of population over a region. This might be done by dividing the region into areas, perhaps on a grid, and identifying all those areas which have less than the normal rural standard of population density. The distance that has to be travelled to each of these 'open' areas could then be measured from any other area and averaged. The average distance that has to be travelled to an 'open' area from any given area can be weighted together with the average distance for all other areas on the basis of their relative population to arrive at a figure for the region as a whole, and this will presumably differ for different distributions of its population. The lowest figure is the one which maximizes access to open space.

Once we possess, for each of the population distributions which are feasible in terms of the procedure described earlier, measures of its characteristics as regards congestion or access to open space, these can enter as additional restraints which further narrow the range of feasible solutions. For example, we can throw out all solutions which exceed a certain figure for the average distance to 'open' areas. Alternatively we can find the solution which minimizes this, or the one which minimizes aggregate congestion costs for the region. The search for a solution which is optimal in either of these senses would be laborious, but for the fact that a systematic method of conducting it lies to hand in the techniques of linear programming. The problem does not end there, however, because we are unlikely to be able to say that there is one thing above all others which ought to be minimized. Is it more important to minimize congestion costs or to minimize the distance which must be travelled to 'open' areas? We cannot say. And so we come back in the end to the necessity of choice. But at least we should be able to choose in knowledge rather than ignorance of its effects.

The usefulness of the sort of model which I have described hinges upon the possibility of finding for the UK stable and significant statistical relationships to express the mutual attraction for each other of the geographical sub-units into which regions may be divided. This needs much investigation, whose results will no doubt throw up variables which I have overlooked in the simple formula which I have used. Models invariably become more complicated as they improve, although they do not always improve as they become more complicated. A particular difficulty which has to be faced is that the distances which people will travel to work are probably greater than they would be if the full economic cost of the journey had to be borne by them in every case. We are moving towards this; but as we do so our estimates of the coefficients in the formula that I have used will be biased upwards to the extent that they are based on observations of the past. There will no doubt be other difficulties, which I bequeath to others more competent at model-making than I am.

I began this paper by criticizing institutionism—the idea that problems are solved by setting up institutions, when the prior need is to evolve the conceptual ideas which can define the tasks which institutions can then be designed to tackle. On reflection, it may be that the British preference for institutions over ideas requires that they should be evolved in that order. The reverse order, ideas before institutions, might mean in our climate that nothing was done at all. I hope that I have shown that, for the piece of institutionism exemplified by the regional planning apparatus of the UK, provided that it does not waste its time on matters to which it has little to contribute, there is a proper function and a problem whose solution can be advanced through its establishment.

Index